CW01080300

WHO WILL TELL MY STORY?

WHO WILL TELL MY STORY?

A
GAZA
DIARY

First published by Guardian Faber in 2025
Guardian Faber is an imprint of Faber & Faber Ltd
The Bindery, 51 Hatton Garden
London EC1N 8HN

Guardian is a registered trademark of
Guardian News & Media Ltd,
Kings Place, 90 York Way, London N1 9GU

Typeset by Faber & Faber Limited
Printed and bound in the UK by CPI Group (UK) Ltd,
Croydon CR0 4YY

A CIP record for this book
is available from the British Library

ISBN 978–1783–35327–9

Printed and bound in the UK on FSC® certified paper in line with our continuing
commitment to ethical business practices, sustainability and the environment.
For further information see faber.co.uk/environmental-policy

Our authorised representative in the EU for product safety is
Easy Access System Europe, Mustamäe tee 50, 10621 Tallinn, Estonia
gpsr.requests@easproject.com

2 4 6 8 10 9 7 5 3 1

CONTENTS

Editor's Note
vii

Introduction
1

A GAZA DIARY
17

Notes
283

EDITOR'S NOTE

With permission of the author, minor grammatical and syntactical amendments have been made to this diary. Names and other identifying details have been changed to protect the privacy of individuals and maintain confidentiality.

INTRODUCTION

I never understood the concept of the 'Key of Return', that rotten copper key. It keeps being passed from one Palestinian generation to the next, from those who were forced to leave their homes in 1948 to their children and then their grandchildren. We 'younger' Gazans used to have a joke about it: 'Grandma, if you ever go back to your land and your home, the house will have a multi-lock door. No need for your copper key.'

Up until she died a couple of years ago, my friend's grandmother, who was born, raised and started a family in Nazareth (spelled Al Nasrah in Arabic), had always wished to be buried in her homeland, to see her home one last time. It was a dream that never came true. In her final days she had a very tiny body; she was barely able to move, yet she always did her best to cook for her grandchildren, even though they were in their thirties by then. When I used to visit, she would be sitting in her chair, and she would always share stories of a place that was deeply engraved in her heart. I could see her eyes filled with joy when speaking of her own kitchen, the picnics they had and the different places she left behind.

It took me a very long time to understand how she felt – over thirty-five years, in fact, when I myself was forced to leave my house, my street, my city and my country. After several unbearable, agonising months of displacement in the south of Gaza, I made it to Egypt. My body left, but my heart and soul stayed. Each night in my rented apartment, I go to the closet, check for the pencil case hidden between the clothes and sheets, open it and find the key to my home. It is a key I know has no use since the doors were all broken by the heavy bombing, but each time I look at it I can remind myself that there is hope, a hope that one day I will return to my apartment, to my street, to my loved ones, to my Gaza.

When I was young, I was always eager to learn. The more I learned, the more I wish I hadn't. This year taught me that the term 'identity' goes far beyond the classic definition of a set of qualities, beliefs, traits and appearances that characterise a person. The key to my apartment has become a part of my identity. The places I used to pass through every day in Gaza, on my way to work or to visit a friend, have become a part of who I am. The smells, the scenes, the sounds – they are all an essential part of me.

If you passed by the intersection of Al Nasser and Wehda Streets in Gaza City, you would be tempted by the beautiful smell of baking and bread coming from the Families Bakery. It was established in 1984, forty years ago, and started as a small shop, the owner working with his children to prepare the bread and delivering it using his own car. The bakery got bigger and they added more products, like croissants, sweets and cookies.

When on a diet, passing by the bakery was torture to me. I remember how I used to meet my friends there before heading on somewhere else – what better way to start any journey other than food? I remember my friend falling in love with their doughnuts, but for me it was the plain bread they made. All you needed was a sprinkle of thyme and some olive oil, and you had yourself the most delicious sandwich. The last I heard about the bakery was that the production lines and the solar energy panels were all bombed. The bakery stopped functioning.* The last post on their Facebook page was published on 6 October 2023, wishing their customers a blessed Friday.

Next to the bakery is Abu Talal falafel shop, a small place with a big history. People would stand in long lines waiting for the hot falafel balls to come out of the oil. In my opinion, Abu Talal makes the best falafel, though there is a huge debate among Gazans about who is on top: is it Abu Talal or Al Sousi? Al Sousi falafel shop was established in 1975 in Al Rimal Street, which was developed over the years to become the 'downtown of Gaza', hosting some of the best shops and agencies. That small street shop remained over all those years, and you would see hundreds of people waiting to get their sandwiches before going to work or heading back to their homes after a long day.

During the war, I heard that Al Sousi got back to work in the south, selling falafel on a small street corner, hanging

* The Families Bakery has recommenced its operations at much-reduced and frequently interrupted capacity, with people receiving their bread through a small window rather than being able to enter the shop itself.

up a torn paper sign with the name of the shop. When I went there, I could see the happiness of the dozens of people, those who had money, who were able to buy falafel. I waited for ten minutes but I did not buy any, not because I knew I might have to wait for hours, since they were using wood to generate heat to fry the falafel, but simply because it was not the same place – not the same people, aroma or even feeling.

I was among the lucky ones who were able to leave Gaza and come to Egypt. To this day I am not sure why my life was more precious than all the children, women and men who were stuck in the area of death. I have the blessing to leave, to survive, to live. But am I really living? Egypt is beautiful, but Gazans are traumatised, afraid, worried of the unknown. Despite the millions of Egyptians and people of other nationalities I see, I can easily detect a fellow Gazan. It is not about their appearance nor the accent, but rather the pain that has been engraved in our souls, as if our energies attract each other. That sad, distracted, grieving look is one I never get wrong: it is another Gazan, someone else who lost everything, trying to keep their head above water, trying to live, unsure whether they will be able to.

I rarely go out. I am unable to. I cannot fathom the idea of being in a world that functions normally: employees going to their jobs, children holding their books, the sight of food everywhere. Oh God! There is food everywhere, there is enough food in this world for everyone, yet Gazans are left starving.

When I first arrived in Egypt, I ordered lots of food, and I kept eating even when I was not hungry. Then the opposite

4

happened – I stopped eating. A friend of mine who made it to Egypt with her mother, leaving behind many family members in Gaza, told me that she feels so guilty that she only eats what they eat. If her family in Gaza manages to get a can of beans, she buys a can of beans in Egypt and eats it; if they find wheat and everyone gets half a loaf, she eats half a loaf. 'How can I enjoy the food available here while my loved ones have no food? I cook for my mother, she is sick, but I never touch the food I make. If they eat, I eat. If they don't, then I won't.'

Another friend of mine once sent me a picture that she received from me years ago. It was of three plates of *kunafa* (a type of sweet), and each plate had a different type: Arab, Nabulsi and Istanbul *kunafa*. During the cold weather, I would order three plates and eat them, allowing myself the sugar rush. She told me that she dreams of going to Saqallah or Abu Al Sa'oud, two famous sweet shops in Gaza, to eat some sweets. I replied to her with a photo of the lemon slush from Kazem Ice Cream Shop. I told her that one day we will have sweets together again.

* * *

One type of gathering that I don't miss is farewells. Most of my friends who made it to Egypt and were able to get visas one way or another decided to leave the country.

'There is nothing left. If it were up to me, I wouldn't even think of it, but I don't want my children to face the same misery we have been through. We tried and tried, and you know that. You are the most positive person I have met in my life. Look at you, your energy is gone, your love for life is gone. I cannot jeopardise ruining the lives of my children. They are already scarred for life, but not any more.' Those were the words of my friend, a mother of two beautiful children, aged ten and eight. She was able to escape Gaza with them to Egypt, but not her husband. During her stay in Egypt, her husband lost his dad and couldn't bury him. She managed to get a visa to Australia at the beginning of the war. She waited for months before then making the tough decision to take her children and never look back.

At the end of each gathering I would hug the departing friend, cry and say the same sentence over and over: 'May God rue the war that parted us.' The last farewell gathering was at another friend's rented apartment. He has managed to go to Spain, trying to secure a better life for his wife and daughter. After everyone left, I stayed with them. We spoke about how cruel our world is, how we are unable to understand how the world is sitting there, watching us from afar, witnessing our misery, yet doing nothing. 'My father had two dreams: to build a house and to have his six children with their families around him, to see them around while he grows old.' She told me how he would work day and night as a teacher and private tutor to collect money to provide a good life for them. 'Between private lessons, he would lie on a wooden chair and take medicine for the agonising pain of his back. I would be heartbroken.' Their house is gone, and her siblings are scattered all over the world. She believes they were smarter than her, understanding the reality that

Gaza is not for Gazans. But she wanted to stay, and she did her best to, until she came to understand, too. 'Our house is gone, and neither my parents nor my siblings are gathered in the same place. My father's dream is gone.'

* * *

These diaries were almost not written. When I was approached by my dear mentor and friend, Ruaridh, the one I call 'the small light above my shoulder', I said, 'No, I don't want to write. I am too tired of writing. What change would it bring? What impact would it have?' He did not pressure me, though he made sure to remind me of the importance of writing to inspire, to share knowledge and to bridge gaps.

There are many people I am forever grateful to for being in my life, and Ruaridh is definitely one of them. He kept encouraging me to write. The more I wrote, the more I realised that writing was therapy to me, a way to believe that I matter, to hope that my words might be of some importance to someone living thousands of miles away who hadn't even heard of a place called Gaza.

When possible, and when I had access to the internet and a source of power (which was rare), Ruaridh and I would always exchange emails and WhatsApp messages. On 13 October, I wrote to him: 'At midnight all people in the North and Gaza City were asked to go to the South . . . it was a sleepless night full of tears and fear . . . We had to go separate ways from the family we were with . . . The new place we are in has no electricity or internet . . . and my batteries are off . . . Ruaridh, it is 1948 all over again . . .'

He kept checking on me, guiding me, sending me positive emails, and most importantly, he heard me when I was lost and afraid. There was a period where I had many doubts writing about my own experience, which, no matter how horrible, was better than that of other Gazans, those who had no place to stay, those with daily work and no money saved, those who lost loved ones or parts of their bodies. I was ashamed to express my suffering and sadness while there are others with deeper tragedies.

In another correspondence, I wrote to Ruaridh: 'I think I figured out the secret of good writing: put yourself in a deadly situation, live in constant fear, never let your adrenaline go down, gather ten people around you (have at least two children crying), give yourself a few minutes to write and *voilà*! You got yourself a good piece . . . My heart was literally aching.'

* * *

I am not sure if using the term 'survived' is accurate. I did not survive. My body, physically, to some extent, made it out of Gaza, but that does not mean that I am OK, it does not mean that I am fine, it does not mean that I am the same person as before the war started (especially given that, at the time of writing these words, the war is still ongoing).

Having panic attacks has become a normal experience that Gazans go through. I remember one time having a panic attack in the middle of an extremely busy road, with thousands of cars passing on both sides. My legs could not hold me. I simply fell on the pavement and cried hysterically for half an hour.

The shocking part is that panic attacks can happen while you are asleep. I remember another time waking up and suddenly, immediately after opening my eyes, as if it was a continuation of a long thought process while asleep, I was thinking about what happened to us, the many challenges we were facing and what might happen in the future.

Will we ever go back to Gaza, after losing everything?

Are we going to stay our whole lives in Egypt, while Gaza is right next to us?

Will we be forced to move to a third country?

Do I need to start from scratch?

All my life savings are disappearing, gradually, so what will happen when I don't have any money left?

I know that some of my friends died with their families, but . . . oh God, they actually died! I cannot see them any more. I am lying to myself, acting as if once the war ends, if it does, I will see them. They are dead. Will I ever be able to visit my parents' graves? Are the graves still safe? Were they bombed?

I got out of bed and was terrified. I called a friend of mine, who told me that I was having another panic attack. We talked for an hour. Well, to be specific, I talked for an hour, and she played the role of therapist and calmed me down.

Even simple things can trigger a panic attack. When my friend travelled through two countries to spend a few days with me after almost two years of not having a vacation, she brought me several gifts. Upon arrival she wanted to surprise me, so she asked a friend of hers to call me and ask me to come down. When I did, I saw her with the two plants, one big and one small. We hugged and talked, yet my mind was on the plants: will I be able to take care of them? I have been struggling for over a year now to take care of myself and keep myself alive. Some days it is almost impossible to get out of bed and do normal things like eating – now I am responsible for another living thing? After the first day, I woke up and immediately went to the balcony to check on the plants. Watering them has become a big burden on me. The idea of forgetting to do so brings me stress.

I miss the plants we used to have in my apartment. One of them was taken care of by my mother for a long time, before she passed away. We believe that any good thing, no matter how simple, is counted as a good deed for deceased people. In this case, I have always believed that as long as this plant continued to be taken care of, continued to grow, my mother would be receiving good deeds as well. The plant does not exist now.

I got in a car with my friend, and we began heading towards a restaurant one hour away from us. She was sure I was going to like it, but I couldn't hold back my tears and began crying, and she started crying, too. She begged me to tell her what was going on. 'Every now and then someone I know dies. Every day another dream ends. My soul is dead. We are ruined. I am not sure I can handle this any more. I am so tired and vulnerable and weak.' I told her that I am not alive any more; my body is functioning, but I am dead inside. I told her that I don't want to go out, I don't want to meet new people, I haven't been eating and I don't want to go to a restaurant. She asked the driver to stop, and we got out of the car. We sat by the Nile, on the ground, and spoke for hours.

The Nile is beautiful, but I miss Gaza's sea. In one of his poems, Mahmoud Darwish said:

Gaza is not the most beautiful city.
Its shore is not bluer than the shores of Arab cities.
Its oranges are not the most beautiful in the Mediterranean
   basin.
Gaza is not the richest city.

Its shore is definitely not the bluest, but it is my shore. The sand of the beach has witnessed the many walks I had with my friends, the talks where we expressed our inner-most thoughts, sometimes laughing and sometimes crying. There was a cafe by the sea that my friends and I would meet at from time to time. We would bring our lunch with us, play games and take lots of photos. One time, during Ramadan, we decided to have *iftar* (breaking the fast) in that cafe, so we ordered food and gathered about one hour before Maghreb prayer. The food came too late, however, and half of the order was missing. I remember my Christian friends quickly got in the car and promised not to return without food. We were hungry, yet no one among those who had received their meals wanted to eat before the others. After forty minutes, our friends returned with victorious smiles, raising their hands to show us the food they brought. We welcomed them as heroes!

11

It is true that Gaza is not the most beautiful city, but it is the city where many confessed their love for the first time, where children enjoyed their childhood making and flying kites, where people started their businesses and experienced success. Gaza holds within its layers millions of stories that deserve to be told.

The Gaza I know has mosques and churches next to each other. The church of St Porphyrius, the oldest church in Gaza, shares a wall with a mosque. You would see the big cross of the church in line with the mosque's minaret. The Gaza I know has many Muslims who celebrate Christmas and the lighting of the tree in the YMCA. The Gaza I know has witnessed Christians who would fast all Ramadan in solidarity with their Muslim friends, breaking their fasts together. During the horrible days of the war, the church hosted both Christians and Muslims who had fled their homes looking for safety. Unfortunately, St Porphyrius was bombed, and so was the oldest mosque in Gaza, Al Omari, which was built in the fifth century.

While walking with my friend, she told me how much she missed her Christmas tree back in her home in Gaza. I told her about my tree as well. We are both Muslims, but the tree was a cornerstone of our houses from December to February. Two days later, Google Photos shared with me an old selfie I had taken next to my tree. I sent it to my friend.

Google Photos has become, in one way or another, a history book. One of my friends used to get annoyed by how many photos I used to take. Now that everyone in our friendship group is in a different place (some still trapped in Gaza, a few in Egypt and the rest in different countries), he thanks me for taking and sending all these photos, because 'they are a reminder of the good times we had together. I never thought that we would never get the chance to have a similar gathering.'

*   *   *

Another form of history is created through embroidery, or *tatreez* in Arabic. For centuries, women have used this skill to earn money. Gazans and Palestinians have developed a signature look through it, and each city has a unique style – who thought that needles and threads could create magic! You would see Gazan women wearing their embroidered *thobes* (long-sleeved dresses) proudly, showing their culture, showcasing their hand-made, hand-stitched dresses. And when you see a foreigner wearing an embroidered shawl or bag, you know for sure it is a statement of their support and love for Gazans.

In the past, embroidery would also indicate which area a woman came from and her social status: a single woman's dress would be white with lots of shapes; a married woman's dress would include red, orange or yellow threads; a widow would wear a black dress embroidered with green threads. The styles would change, too, in terms of the type of stitch used, the fabric and the drawings created, ranging from orange blossoms, date palms and cypresses to tents, grape-vines and feathers. My favourite is the Canaanite Star motif.

*   *   *

A man I know who remained in Gaza told me that if you walk its streets now, or what is left of them, you would see the corpses of unidentified people, men, women and children who died while trying to find a safe place away from the bombing. He shared videos of places where I had spent most my life, yet they were unrecognisable to me until he told me the locations. He tells me Gaza will never be the same. I think to myself, 'Neither will we.'

Although the war showed us the worst of the world, it also showed us real kindness. During the darkest of times, there were people who managed to help others, feed them and provide them with shelter and a shoulder to cry on when no one else could. Among them is Ahmad's family, who took my sister and me in for a very long period. Even though they had little money and their resources were scarce, they welcomed us. They used to give us food before they themselves had eaten. Ahmad's mother, also referred to in these diaries as the grandmother, was a real example of altruism, mercy and generosity. This family was a gift sent to us from God.

At the beginning of the war, they were strangers whom we had met for the first time, thinking we would stay at their modest house for a couple of days. On the day we left, they were family members, people who have guaranteed a spot in our hearts for the rest of our lives. I hear the news, and I am told by those I know in the south that there is no food, no money, nothing. Yet, when we speak to Ahmad's family, they reply to us in a cheerful tone, telling us they are OK, that they have everything they need. They even say that they are worried about us. The more the vicious monster of war gets its claws deeper into Gazans, the more Ahmad's family shows love and care towards others. I pray for them to be safe and for this nightmare to end.

The war in Gaza is nothing but bitter, but it was those who shared the experience with me who made it less insufferable. This was most true of my sister: once we arrived in Egypt, I hugged her and told her that I wouldn't have survived if it weren't for her. We were a team, thinking together, supporting each other, facing the unimaginable daily struggles. It was true of my friends, too, the ones who happened to be displaced to areas near me. We would work together on securing resources to survive, and we would talk and laugh and play cards to ease the agony and fear we were living through. Also, my therapist, who is not Palestinian, she kept sending me emails on an almost daily basis, sharing positive thoughts, telling me that I would make it out alive. Most of the time I would reply with one short message: 'Still alive.' And then my non-Gazan friends, who would check on me day and night. There were many times when death was so close, and I would ask them to do a charitable thing on my behalf if I died. All of them would tell me one thing: 'You will live.'

I ask myself now: why am I still writing? I am writing because, just like the key to my apartment, the photos of me and my friends in Gaza, the embroidery dresses and every shop and institute in Gaza, these diaries are a symbol and a confirmation. A symbol of love, survival and the desire to live, and a belief that no matter where we end up, regardless of all the misery and agony we have been through, we will never stop dreaming of going back to Gaza. It will always remain in our hearts.

Please, keep the Gazans in your positive thoughts and prayers, and thank you for reading these diaries.

8–10 December 2024

A GAZA DIARY

Saturday 7 October

6 a.m. I wake up thinking about my tennis session. Tennis, don't I sound fancy! This year I decided to take care of my mental and physical health. This means no stress, no negative energy and definitely more tennis.

I check my mobile to see what else I have scheduled. A visit to the doctor and some errands. I see a message from my friend telling me it seems we won't meet for tennis. There is a 'situation'. As a Gazan, there is no confusion about what is meant. An escalation. Again.

How many times do we have to go through this? Since 2000, it has been going on, non-stop, leaving more bruises on our souls and taking away big chunks of our lives. Clichéd, isn't it? But that is the only way to describe the impact of what has been happening. Gazans are walking trauma vessels . . . living in constant fear for their lives and futures.

I wash my face and try to check the news. The internet connection is bad. A thought pops into my head and I start frantically searching the flat. My sister looks confused: 'What are you looking for?'

'The apartment ownership contract,' I say. 'I need to find it. If our building gets bombed, I need evidence that this apartment belongs to me.'

Having keys to the apartment is not enough; living in this apartment for years is not enough, either. When I find the contract, I relax a bit. It is amazing how accustomed we have gotten to misery. Death and bombs are the first thoughts that come to our minds when a 'situation' starts.

I sit on my chair, look at my messages and wonder – what will we lose this time? What part of our soul, if any is left, will be broken? Which of my friends will lose their lives? Or will it be me? Will it be me?

If I hadn't been Palestinian, I would have wanted to be Finnish. I read once that Finland is the happiest place on Earth. I want to be happy, where all I care about is my health and my tennis session.

Sunday 8 October

8 p.m. I am thirsty. I can't find the bottle of water I thought I had in the flat.

I receive a text from a friend: 'The night has come. I am terrified. Will we be able to witness another morning?' Gazans are most terrified of the night hours, when most of the bombing takes place. My sister reminds me to slightly open the windows because a nearby attack could shatter the glass. I tell my friend to stay hopeful. I am a hypocrite – asking people to be optimistic in times where nothing is certain. I keep forgetting to drink water.

11 p.m. I am thirsty, I need something to drink.

We have packed our essentials in case we need to flee. We have the two carriers to put our cats in. 'What about the fish?' I say to my sister. As heavy bombing goes on, not knowing where the explosions are coming from, my sister and I start thinking of creative ways to save the fish. Believe it or not, it is a family member, and it has survived a lot with us. If asked to evacuate, we wonder if we could hold the small water tank in our hands, but no, we live on one of the upper floors and we will be panicking, running down the stairs. The tank might break. After a lot of deliberation, our tired brains – with no sleep in thirty-six hours – decide we will use a plastic jar with a lid. We make small holes in the top and fill it with water. We have a plan.

Monday 9 October

1 a.m. Complete darkness, no electricity, where did I put the water bottle? I really need something to drink.

I can hear the neighbours outside arguing. Apparently, one of them still has some bread and was offering it to the other, who was too embarrassed to take it and offered to pay him for it. Gazans are weird. We would offer you the last bit of food we have. Some bakeries are still working, but everyone is terrified of going into the street to buy essentials. No place is safe, no one is safe.

2.30 a.m. I find the bottle of water.

A message from a friend abroad asking if I am getting enough sleep. I tell her that the bombing keeps us awake. She says how sorry she is, and then shares an idea. I am 100 per cent sure she thinks it is helpful. 'Why don't you wear earpieces? You can sleep then.'

People sympathise, but they cannot relate to what you are going through. My friend does not understand that bombing is not about the noises, it is about the possibility of sudden death. Without saying goodbye to our loved ones, before completing the projects we started, before hugging those we care about and asking for their forgiveness. She knows, but definitely doesn't realise, the severity of the situation. I choose not to respond to the text.

5 a.m. We have survived another night. Every inch of my body aches – lack of sleep is a torture. My throat is dry. I look at the untouched water bottle . . . I really need to drink.

Later I've had to evacuate my home.

The message came on the building's WhatsApp group. I stood up calmly and told my sister it was our time. 'The whole area needs to evacuate.' No other communication was shared, we knew what to do, we have planned for this.

I went to grab the younger cat, who is easier to catch. I put her in the carrier by the door. My sister went for the bigger one. She caught it after some effort and put it in the other carrier. She took the fish out of the tank and put it in the plastic jar with holes on top. Then we went to the door, grabbed the bags with our legal documents, passports and essentials, and left.

I live in a multi-storey building, with four apartments on each level. I have never really interacted with any of the residents. I mostly see people by the elevator, and we exchange polite smiles before going behind our own doors.

People were running down the stairs. A man was holding two children while his wife was dragging a small suitcase, and their teenage daughter, tears running down her eyes, was yelling: 'I don't want to leave . . . I don't want to leave.'

I asked my sister: 'Did you put the fish in the jar?'

'Yes.'

'Did you pick it up?'

'I thought you got it.'

I put the key back in the door, unlocked it, and my sister ran inside, got the fish and we left. We did our best to run in between the many people going down. A couple of women were running, yet talking.

'But where will we go?'

'Anywhere, we'll think about it later.'

We reached the street and everyone started going in different directions. People were getting angry with each other; some were crying, some were confused. We stopped in the middle of the street and started phoning friends.

The first we called was also evacuating. The second welcomed us.

Later still We reach their house, exhausted. They live on the seventh floor, and the lift isn't working because there is no electricity.

Our friends are a family of nine – husband, wife, six children and the grandmother. They are sleep-deprived, you can see how tired and afraid they all are. They welcome us with weak smiles. They offer us coffee and cookies stuffed with dates.

We all sit there, coffee and sweets untouched, and face the long night ahead.

The mother calls her brother, who lives on our street, where we had just evacuated from. He is heading to another sibling's house for refuge. She worries that he and his family haven't arrived there yet. She asks him to call her the minute they do.

Sitting between her youngest children, a boy of four and a girl of six, I wonder about the sad life ahead of them, the many escalations they will witness – if they are lucky enough to survive this one. I ask her: 'How are your children doing?'

'They are coping well and they don't feel afraid when there is bombing, especially Nour.' She says the word 'especially' in a way that I could tell she wasn't being honest. She asks the children to go inside and then she tells me, in a lowered voice, that her daughter is terrified.

The bombs start. Evacuating our block means that we are out of the extreme danger of a targeted area; it does not mean that we are safe.

With the first airstrike the building shakes, the pressure outside is so strong that wind pushes out the curtains. Nour starts screaming, she goes to her mother and holds tight. A series of strikes follow and all of us sit holding on tight to our seats, flinching with every hit. The mother is patting Nour's shoulder, saying: 'Everything is going to be OK.'

Once the bombs stop, she asks her middle daughter to take the children and prepare sandwiches for them. When they disappear, she says: 'I am so worried about her, she is very afraid.'

I tell her that I think expressing fear is the healthy thing. The fact that the rest of us, including the four-year-old, remained silent is unhealthy and shows our trauma. The other children are focused on their phones, checking on their friends.

A couple of hours later, the eldest son comes and says that his uncle's building, the one who lives near to us, was destroyed. We are in shock. The mother starts calling friends of her brother to find out if he knows or not. She starts crying, while asking them to support him and never leave him alone. She speaks about how hard he worked to buy his apartment and on renovating it.

I feel extremely sorry for his loss and terrified that my building will be next. Her husband and the children are sitting around her, all quiet. Then I see Nour pat her mother's shoulder and tell her: 'Everything is going to be OK, Mama, everything is going to be OK.'

Tuesday 10 October

I haven't slept in four days.

It is not for the lack of trying; I did my best to close my eyes and just relax. Then the airstrikes hit, and I find myself jumping off whatever I am sleeping on – a mattress on the floor at our friend's home or an uncomfortable chair at the second friend's home we shifted to after.

The nights are terror, and once the light of dawn comes, the adrenaline of survival kicks in and the new day starts. Watching the news, talking to loved ones, complaining about the poor internet connection and no electricity.

'We were told we will get four hours of electricity a day. Almost two days have passed and nothing has happened,' the lady we are staying with says.

People in Gaza have used many solutions to the electricity problem over the years, including backup batteries for charging phones, LED lights and the internet router. Electricity generators for part-rental became widespread, with people paying eight times the price of normal electricity. This, of course, is only for those with the ability to pay. During the 'escalation', the generator owner provided electricity for a few hours, aware of the shortage of fuel and the possibility of fuel cuts.

Every inch of my body aches, but I am irritated. I have this urge to scream, yet I am too exhausted.

'Would you like to shower?' my friend asks me.

Oh my God! I haven't showered in four days. Another reason I'm irritated. Usually, when you go to other people's homes for refuge, taking a shower is off the table. It is enough that they are hosting you, feeding you and keeping you 'safe'.

The second family we are staying with is an extended one. One lot lives on the second floor, where we are, and the others on the fifth. We all gather on the second floor at night because it is easier to flee, if we have to, and – I'm never sure if this is accurate or not – it's supposedly safer than upstairs.

9 p.m. The bombing has broken the bathroom door on the second floor. So I need to shower on the fifth floor. The others are worried – taking a shower at night could be risky.

They all looked at me while I gathered my stuff, as if I were an astronaut preparing his equipment to go to outer space (in my case it was boxers, undershirt and a shirt – I wasn't going to change my shorts because I have only one pair with me). I had lots of advice.

'Stay close to the stairs and avoid the windows.'

'Do it fast, no more than five minutes.'

'Keep your clothes next to you so you can grab them fast if a bombing happens.'

I was less afraid and more excited – a shower!

I took my shower very quickly and dried my body with the towel that smelled of coconut freshener. After finishing, I vowed that I would never, ever buy a coconut freshener so I wouldn't remember these days.

I go down, feeling better, and despite all the chaos around, I lay my body over a couch and sleep for a couple of hours. It is great.

Wednesday 11 October

I am grateful my mother is dead.

Since she died, I have been through a journey of healing and self-reflection. It is weird how the loss of your loved ones opens your heart to many truths and realisations.

Now, amid the destruction, memories of my mother keep coming. Some funny and some sad. At the house of the first family we took refuge at, the woman told us how much she loved my mother. They were our next-door neighbours for seven years, and she would spend many of her days at our house with her young children. Once, she lost count of time and stayed till 7 p.m.

She said: 'I will never forget how my husband knocked on your door, and he looked at me and said, "I think you need to pack your bags and go live with them."'

In the past twenty-five years my mother rarely left home but, somehow, she managed to establish some solid friendships.

4 a.m. Awake.

Someone says: 'It is better that your mother did not witness these horrible days we are going through.' I believe this. I am grateful that my mother did not have to go through another escalation, to feel the fear and to be evacuated from her home.

My mother's safety used to be my big worry. She was an elderly, overweight woman who could barely walk. One time, there was bombing and everyone in the building evacuated, but we used to live on the fourth floor, so there was no time to go down the stairs at her pace. I remember her sitting on her couch, with me covering her body with mine, telling her that she will be safe.

Is my mother safe now? In the past, a graveyard in Gaza was bombed. Will the graveyard where my mother is buried be bombed? Will I be able to go and cover her grave with my body and tell her she will be safe?

I miss my mother a lot.

Thursday 12 October

'I lost track of my family; it was very dark, and the bombing was everywhere. My daughter and I kept walking, barefoot, until we reached my aunt's house. The next day, I found out that my family were being hosted by a family we don't know. They saw them fleeing and welcomed them into their home.'

My friend Samar is on the phone. Airstrikes had targeted a location near her house.

Samar is everyone's friend. She is the one you go to when you need guidance or support. She was contacting every-one to check on them and make sure they were fine. She is forty-four, with a seventeen-year-old daughter, but looks twenty-five. One time, we agreed that her motto in life should be 'getting wiser yet looking younger'.

She tells me she wants to go back to her house to collect their things. She had never had to evacuate in the previous escalations, so I find myself giving her guidance for once.

'Here is what you need to take with you . . .' As I speak, I feel the sensation that I am too accustomed to this. It breaks my heart that this good person, who is kind to everyone, is facing this horrible situation.

'Your medicine, take as much as you can. Money, pass-ports. Clothes – pack extra underwear. Tissues. Your house keys – never miss those, I was about to drop mine when we evacuated. Deodorant, toothbrush, your laptop, charger and power bank . . .'

I feel silence on the other side. I'm afraid we have lost the connection.

'Samar, are you there?'

'Yes. It is just overwhelming.'

Then she says: 'There is a small box I keep some precious things in, like my daughter's first dress and some letters. I will take it. You know what else it has? Do you remember that time when all our group went out to the ice cream shop? We took a napkin and we all signed our names on it? You laughed at us and said this is what teenagers do. I still have it, and I will take it.'

I feel helpless not being able to go help my friend. I think about why a seventeen-year-old girl was running barefoot for her life in the middle of the night.

I wish Samar good luck and hang up.

In Gaza, men don't cry. Since childhood, boys are taught not to cry because they are *men* and tough. Growing up, they realise that expressing their feelings is rarely welcomed, and if they do, they will be judged and categorised as feminine (never a bad thing!). They become adults acquainted with the habit of bottling their emotions.

During these devastating times, I try to stay in touch with my friends. My female friends share their sadness, fear and all ranges of emotions they have. My male friends exchange few words. 'I am fine.' 'Good.' 'The situation is bad.' 'Such-and-such is expected to happen.' Even when I encourage them to share more, they don't.

By Gaza standards, I belong to the 'soft' side of the masculinity spectrum. I cry and never feel ashamed. This has caused me a lot of problems. However, I have to admit that when we evacuated the first time, I did benefit from the pressure that our society puts on men to never express themselves.

It had been a very long day, with people talking, screaming and crying in the street. The family we went to were worried and they had received bad news. There was the non-stop chaos in my head. Late at night, and with the continuous, terrifying bombing, the host wife, her children and mother-in-law decided to go to the basement for more safety; my sister went with them. Upstairs, the husband, the oldest son and I stayed in the apartment.

You could tell that each of us had a lot going on; our eyes said a lot. However, for four hours we barely spoke, it was like a silent pact. We were either following the news, looking at our mobiles, reading something or looking at the empty space ahead of us. The husband made himself a snack and ate it. The bombing went on, the building we were in was shaking right and left, yet we remained silent. We were tired, consumed with our thoughts and, most importantly, silent. I really needed that.

We have had to move to another house. We finally found a driver who would take us. I begged him to pass by our street to see if our building is still standing. All night we heard nothing but rumours about where the bombing was.

Instead of ten minutes, it took the taxi driver half an hour to reach our street. The destruction was unbelievable, like being in an end-of-the-world action movie.

The car was moving very slowly on roads filled with destroyed buildings, cables and rocks. Objects, or what was left of them, were appearing in slow motion. I saw one collapsed building with three men standing opposite, looking at it, and heavy tears were falling down from their eyes.

Men in Gaza do cry.

When they lose their homes that they spent their whole lives building, they cry.

When they see their dreams and hopes getting destroyed, they cry.

When they realise how scary and uncertain their future is, they cry.

And because they are human beings, full of feelings and emotions, they cry.

Friday 13 October

3 a.m. I manage to sleep for a couple of hours. Last night, there was no internet connection; even the mobile data was very bad. With eyes half open, I check my phone and see many messages from people saying that residents of north Gaza and Gaza City should move south. The adrenaline starts, my heart is beating fast. In no time, my eyes are wide open and I get out of bed.

4 a.m. My sister and I sit at the kitchen table with the couple who are hosting us. We need to discuss the situation: should we leave or should we stay? The wife prepares coffee for them and a cup of Earl Grey for me.

'So, what are our options? Leave and stay at one of the schools? Do you know what happens there? There will be hundreds, if not thousands, of people.'

'We could stay. We are civilians. This is our home – we are not harming anyone.'

'We don't know what will happen. Leaving is the safe choice.'

'I will not leave my home. I would prefer to die here rather than in a place I don't belong to.'

'We all have heard about the lack of water, electricity and the basic needs in the shelters. People have fights, and it is just awful.'

The discussion takes hours. We all make a decision: we are not leaving.

8 a.m. I don't believe anyone in Gaza is asleep. By now I have made about fifteen phone calls, asking friends whether they will leave or stay. No unified answer.

I repack my bag to sort out what is important and what I should leave if we change our minds. Passing a mirror, I see my reflection: my eyes are tired and covered by dark circles. I also realise that I have lost weight.

10 a.m. Everyone is leaving, except for us.

People are panicking, and the theories about what might happen are horrifying. We're discussing all possible scenarios.

'We can leave for a couple of days and see what happens.'

'My friend, who said she wouldn't leave, called and said that she and her husband had changed their minds.'

'I'm afraid if we stay, horrible things will happen.'

Suddenly, the wife stands up and says: 'You want me to die in a place I don't know . . . to spend the last days of my life humiliated? We can stay here and nothing bad will happen.' Then she stops for a minute, tears falling, and says: 'I have a feeling that if I leave, I am never coming back.'

We decided, by a majority of votes, that we are leaving.

11 a.m. We are seven people, one car, four suitcases and five backpacks. The car doesn't fit all of us. We need another, but there are none available.

My sister, who is very nervous, calls everyone she knows. She does not ask for a car, she demands a car. I calmly try contacting everyone I think can help. Neither of us succeed.

36

Where to go? Going into a school, hospital or shelter is not an option. The husband starts calling his friends to see if someone has an apartment we could rent or crash in.

Finally, the husband says: 'We could go to our land. It is empty, but we can stay there until we figure out what to do.'

Everyone knows that is not a good option. It takes us back to the same old conversation: should we stay or leave?

We decide to stay. Then I start crying. I am afraid, terrified, confused.

Finally, a decision is made: my sister and I decide to leave, and the family decide to stay.

My sister finds us a place to stay, and my friends help us to get a taxi driver, who gives a ride to two families from Gaza City to Rafah and then comes back for us.

1 p.m. My sister and I hug the family one by one, all of us sobbing. We do not know who has made the right decision. We say our goodbyes. We ask for each other's forgiveness.

They ask us to take the suitcase in which we packed the food and water – since we thought we were going together, we put all of it in one suitcase. We refuse to take it and leave it with them.

1.30 p.m. The scene of the cars evacuating is horrifying. It is group migration. There are many people walking while carrying their children and their bags because they couldn't find a car. Some people are leaving in buses, and others in the backs of trucks. Whenever they see people walking, they invite them to jump in. It breaks my heart leaving.

3 p.m. We arrive. This is the third family that has hosted us since the beginning of the escalation. A family of ten: husband and wife, three children, the wife and three children of the oldest son, and the great-grandfather. They are very nice, simple people who have opened their doors to us, offered us food.

4 p.m. We hear that the husband of the previous family has found an apartment. They have decided to leave.

The night is approaching, and I am scared. When there is bombing at night, Amani, a colleague, always tries to take my mind off the fear. The building will be shaking right and left, and she will send me something like: 'What is your favourite book? Which culture do you like the best?'

Sometimes I play along, pretend I don't know why she is doing this, and answer her questions. Other times I just look at the messages and don't answer.

Saturday 14 October

3 a.m. The first day after our third evacuation. The night in the area we are in is calm, but I can't sleep. I keep waking up with every little sound. I don't just open my eyes, but raise the top part of my body as well to see if everything is OK. I check my mobile and see the weather app sharing the weather in Berlin. It seems that I clicked on something by mistake. I think about how wonderful it would be if I were there, but I am in Gaza.

6 a.m. After some on/off sleep, I wake up and notice that my jaw is hurting. I realise that I've been clenching my teeth. I hear the doorknob moving, and a little face appears: Laila, the youngest in the family. She wants to see the new people sleeping in her house.

I smile at her, and two other heads appear above hers: her older brother and sister, Hamed and Radwa. I invite them in, and they sit next to me on the mattress on the floor, next to the couch where my sister is sleeping. I ask them what they want to be in the future.

'I want to be a nanny,' Laila says.

'I want to be a police officer,' Hamed says.

'I want to be a doctor,' Radwa says.

I am glad to hear their answers. Despite all the horrific things happening around them, they still have hope and dreams for the future. In times like these, hope for a better future is really precious.

8 a.m. The grandmother comes to say hello. She is only forty-three years old; she tells us she had her first baby at sixteen. We speak about the situation, and how some people are abusing others. She tells me: 'Some family members of mine were fleeing from Gaza to the south. The drivers were asking for more than triple the price to take them. They said they were jeopardising their lives and they deserved it.'

Laila shows up again and sits in her grandmother's lap. She asks every morning if she will go to the kindergarten. 'She feels sad when I tell her no. She wants to see her friends and play with them.'

For children it is troubling. A friend tells me how her twelve-year-old daughter's best friend was killed. 'I cannot imagine what the mother of the girl is feeling,' she says. 'My daughter wanted to speak to her, but I asked to let me talk to her first. I thought I would be strong, but both of us started crying. The worst thing a mother could go through is losing her child.'

9 a.m. The whole family is sitting with us. They are the nicest people, but we are tired, so not the best at conversation. I wonder what my friends who are staying at shelters and schools are feeling in those chaotic, noisy situations with zero privacy. I remind myself: you are privileged.

Over tea and coffee, everyone starts sharing stories. Fadel, the oldest son and a father of three, says: 'After the 2014 escalation, I was desperate. I decided to go on one of the illegal boats to reach Europe. My parents forced me not to, but my friend went. The boat never made it, and till this moment we know nothing about him.'

Ahmad, the middle son, doesn't stop taking phone calls. He tells us so many friends and acquaintances have reached out to him to find them places to rent or stay. 'There are no spaces left,' he says. 'Within the last twenty-four hours, some families have found themselves hosting more than fifty people. It is either this or going to the schools and shelter areas.'

The grandmother shares the story of a Palestinian family that has been living in a foreign country for more than twenty years, but decided to come to Gaza for a long holiday. Now, they are stuck.

10 a.m. Ahmad asks me if I want to charge my mobile. I am ecstatic, because I know for sure they have no water, no electricity and no internet. But there are two things I learn: they are cooperative and they are problem-solvers.

For the internet, they asked a neighbour to share his password. We can barely 'catch' the network, but having some internet connection is better than none. As for the electricity, another family at the end of the street have installed solar panels, and all the houses in the street are going to them for charging. We give him our mobile phones, power banks, laptops and a tablet. It takes a long time to manage all the devices, but waiting for a couple of hours without electronic devices is better than being without them the whole time.

As for water, they had a well, but needed a generator to bring the water up. The whole neighbourhood started searching, until they found an old, broken one that they brought to someone to fix. It took him two days. Now, they have water.

Noon One of my cats is next to me. I rub her head and tell her that I'm very sorry they have to go through this with us.

My sister looks at me and says: 'I have been thinking about the same topic, but not about the cats, about us. Why had our father never thought about raising us abroad when he had the chance? He wanted us to be in Gaza . . . the dream! Now, he is dead and we are suffering.'

The fish we brought from home in the plastic container has died.

3 p.m. We hear horrible stories from friends about what is happening in shelters and school areas, where there are thousands of people with no other place to go. We hear about the fights; the lack of food, water and mattresses; how some people are stealing from others; and about harassment.

We start thinking about what to do if we have to evacuate for a fourth time. Just thinking about it stresses me out to the maximum. I receive a phone call from a friend who fled yesterday but is now looking for a new place. 'We are more than seventy people at my aunt's house, and new members are coming soon,' he says. 'Some of the guys decided to leave to give a chance to the newcomers to find a place.'

I try my best to help, asking our host family to ask around and sharing with him the information I get back . . . but nothing works.

5 p.m. My friend, a social worker who had her first baby three weeks ago, cries on the phone to me. 'I never think we will be able to get over this at all,' she says. 'I cannot believe that I fled with my husband and child to one place while my mother and siblings are in another. Will we tell our story or will other people share it after we are gone?'

I say to her firmly: 'Listen to me, you are going to get out of it. Not because of you, but because of your child. He needs his mother to be there with him in every stage of his life, and there are many great memories to come.'

7 p.m. The weather goes from cool in the morning to really hot during the day, and then it becomes really cool in the evening. My sister says: 'Thank God this escalation did not happen in midsummer. We would have suffered way more.'

I look at her and say: 'I wonder what the weather in Berlin is like now.'

Sunday 15 October

3 a.m. I have time to think. To count my blessings. I have been blessed enough to have a good paying job. This has made my life during these times easier, or to be more accurate, less difficult. On day one, I withdrew some cash and kept it with me.

At the beginning, paying extra money did the trick when the shops were emptied of most products, and we were able to get delivery men to bring food. Also, we were able to pay for water. When we moved to the second house, their makeshift battery (used for basic lighting and internet router charging) stopped working, so we got a new one within two days.

Those without money suffered more. Losing electricity meant that fridges stopped working and stored food was damaged. It meant no air conditioning nor fans in the heat. And as for the water, it goes without saying: washing, cleaning and showering are off the table.

The price of vegetables has doubled. What do people do? The price of power packs has gone up 70 per cent. We have bought them and so are able to have access to phones. For others, it's hit and miss.

Hamdi, the janitor at the second house we evacuated to, had good relations with the janitor in the next building, which had an internal generator, so he was able to get an electricity line to charge the UPS battery. Residents went down to his room at night to charge their phones.

Being the gatekeeper to the source of electricity, Hamdi became a boss. He started giving orders, expressing clear annoyance when someone asked to charge their phone. He started dealing with less respect with the others.

It is true that all Gazans are suffering, but it is important to recognise the blessings we have during these tough times.

'I can never imagine my naked dead body lying in the street,' Ruba, one member of the second family we stayed with, answered when I asked her why she sleeps fully clothed and wearing a headscarf.

Her brother told me that the night before we joined them, they were told a nearby building would be bombed, so all the residents started running to leave. Ruba took about five extra minutes to get fully clothed.

I couldn't understand how someone can care about what they are wearing in times like these, and I told her the story behind an Arabic proverb: 'Those who were shy are dead.' Once, a huge fire started in a hammam [a Turkish public bath]. Those who did not mind running out naked survived, while the ones who were shy died.

All Gazans are suffering, but for women the situation is worse. As people flee their houses and move in with friends or relatives, women find themselves obliged to wear full scarves and coverings at all times in the presence of male visitors, while also having to prepare food, be good hosts and deal with the children crying out of fear or wanting to play when they cannot go out.

Women are not only facing the horrible situation, but are also the glue that holds families together.

7 p.m. I read the messages from Rola and Ayham, two of my friends abroad. If I miss a text, they panic. I keep reminding them that we don't have access to the internet all the time.

Sometimes they send me audio messages, crying, telling me that they feel useless for not being able to take me out of this situation; sometimes they send me jokes and hopeful notes. One time, they started sending messages, back to back, about what we will do together when all of this is over.

Ayham: 'We will travel together. I will take you to Italy.'

Rola: 'I will invite you to our house to eat my mother's delicious food.'

Ayham: 'We will go bowling, and just like the last time, I will win.'

Rola: 'We will go together to all the bookshops in the world.'

I read their messages, smiling and crying. I prepare for another dark night.

*　　*　　*

My sister receives a phone call from her friend who is living abroad. With the poor internet connection, our loved ones are making international calls just to check on us. They talk for almost an hour, both of them crying. Their conversation is mainly about the guilt my sister's friend is feeling due to being away from her, and my sister telling her how much stronger she feels because of her support.

For the first fifteen minutes, I am sympathetic and grateful my sister has wonderful friends during these times. For the second fifteen minutes, I start reflecting on my own experience and the wonderful friends I have. After half an hour of continuous crying, I am praying for this sadness fest to come to an end. I want to close my eyes and get some sleep.

Once my sister is done, she is still very sad. For no reason, I look up and notice the ceiling light. 'This is the ugliest ceiling light I have ever seen in my life,' I say.

My sister starts laughing, and so do I.

We have had only minutes of sleep when we hear a huge explosion. A house nearby has been bombed. We wake up, terrified, put the cats into their carriers and quickly put the bags by the door to leave immediately if we have to.

For the next two hours I do not stop shaking. I am so cold that I cover myself with the heavy blanket the family gave us, which I had put aside, thinking I wouldn't use it. I want to vomit, but I try to stay calm and still.

No place is safe, and no one is safe. Yet, minutes after the bombing, the grandmother prepares coffee and tea for us and asks if we need some cookies.

The internet connection is really bad. Once every three or four hours I receive some notifications and WhatsApp messages. Nothing else is opening (Facebook, videos, etc.). I see a notification from an application called Anghami (the Arabic version of Spotify), telling me that my weekly mixtape is ready! This is a collection of recommended songs based on the songs you have already played. I smile sarcastically and think that nowadays I am listening to a different soundtrack: bombing.

The room my sister and I are sharing is a small living room, with couches and small tables. At night the family bring us a mattress, some pillows and two covers in case someone would like to sleep on the floor. The room is next to a small balcony that we rarely open: the houses here are so close together that using it would feel like an infringement of their privacy. And, of course, sitting on balconies is dangerous.

We do open the balcony door from time to time for ventilation. This morning, the younger cat ran on to the balcony after an insect, before I was able to stop it. Going outside to catch it, I feel the sun on my skin for the first time in a long while.

I am not a summer person. I hate the sun, and for the past three months I have been using sunscreen religiously. Yet this time I held the cat and tilted my face to enjoy the sun's rays. It felt like a hug.

Radwa, the eldest granddaughter, enters the room. I ask her how she is doing and notice that she looks pale. I wonder if she is sick, but she answers, looking at the ground, ashamed: 'No, I am afraid.' I immediately respond: 'I am afraid, too.' She looks at me, surprised. I am sure that she can tell that the adults around her are afraid, but all of them act as if they are not. I continue: 'We are going through a very tough period. It is OK to feel scared.' She smiles at me in what I think is a grateful manner.

I find out later that her grandmother performs something we call the 'fear-cutting' technique in Arabic on her grandchildren. Fear-cutting is a massage using olive oil done on certain parts of the body where it is believed fear is absorbed. The goal is to get rid of all the knots created due to fear. People of all ages use it.

The youngest child (not grandchild) is sixteen years younger than his oldest brother (the father of the three kids). He is a very nice kid. When we first arrived, he heard me talking about reading and started asking me about the books I love to read and whether I could recommend some writers to him.

Earlier today, I noticed that he was anxious and fully dressed. Usually, in times like these, women wear praying clothes because they are easier to move in, and men stay in their pyjamas. His middle brother was dressed up, too. I asked where they were going, and he said: 'His school friend is at the hospital. His parents and one of his sisters are dead. My brother is terrified, and he wants to visit his friend.'

When they come back, hours later, the teenager comes and sits quietly in the room. My sister and I try to open a conversation and ask how his friend is feeling. He says: 'He is doing very well. He has several wounds, but the doctor says that everything will be OK.' I want him to express his feelings, so I share with him that he looks worried. He says: 'There is something. He does not know that his parents and sister are dead. The doctor asked us not to share

49

the news with him in order for his medical state not to worsen.'

I am losing track of time. Every now and then, I have to ask someone what day or date it is. Most of the time the other person will have to check their phone before replying. I cannot believe that more than a week has passed since the beginning of the escalation.

One of the sons draws my attention to the fact that I am about to take the same medicine for the third time within two hours.

With our friends and family members living outside Gaza, we exchange long messages and detailed phone calls. However, for friends in Gaza, most communication is limited to a word or two:

'OK?'

'Yes.'

'Updates plz.'

'We're fine. You?'

And so on.

In a way, I feel that all we need to know is whether the other person is still alive or not.

Monday 16 October

6 a.m. Several Gazan families I know have decided to go back to the north. Some of them couldn't tolerate staying away from their homes; others couldn't handle the difficult circumstances they had to live in. We decide to stay; it is not safe. One guy I know decided to leave alone after his family refused to go.

8 a.m. My muscles are weak; my knuckles and knees hurt. Sleeping for short periods gives you enough energy to wake up, but you remain tired all day long, unable to sleep again or think properly.

10 a.m. 'Do you need us to send you money?' Since the beginning of the escalation, this is the most frequent question we are asked. Luckily, we do not. What we need is for all this to be over, for us to go to our homes and sleep in our beds. The middle son of the host family, who is studying at university, says: 'If this is over, I will go to the university every day without complaining.'

It makes me realise how fortunate I am. The fact that in these times we don't need money shows how much of a better position we are in, when so many people cannot afford to get their basic needs.

Noon The situation is relatively calm, so we decide to venture out to get some things for the house. I feel surprised seeing the long queue to buy bread. We do not need bread since the grandmother bakes at home using a mud baker (like an oven, but made from mud). There are no water bottles left in the shops.

On our way back, I see a man holding a cat from the street. I am terrified he might hurt it. He takes the cat to a chair on the pavement where he was sitting, and from a plastic bag he takes out some mortadella and feeds it to the cat. In addition, many shops open their doors for people to charge their phones. I am glad to see these simple acts of kindness.

2 p.m. One of the sons of the host family tells me about a big fight that started in the area. After an airstrike, people went to help get injured people out. They immediately covered any dead body out of respect. One man wanted to uncover the body of a young girl whose head had exploded to take a picture of it. The people fought with him and were about to hit him for what he was doing.

I don't understand why, when there is bombing, people all go to the site. People should run away, not towards it. Sometimes they might cause more harm than good, even if the intention is to help.

Since the escalation, I have done my best not to check the internet. In addition to not having a proper connection, I do not want what little is left of my mental health to be ruined. The images, horrible stories and rumours shared online are just awful. However, no matter how much I try, some posts pop up. The ones that break my heart the most are about kids. One post spoke about a mother who was fleeing with her family; she wrote the names and contact information on her children's hands in case they got lost. The other was about two siblings, less than five years old, who were found lost on their own. I believe that eventually they will be reunited with their family, or at least identified.

Another excruciating thing is people who are abroad while their families are in Gaza. I saw a message from a friend in Germany who is studying pharmacy. He had been unable to reach his family, who had fled. He was panicking. I told him communication is very difficult, even between people in Gaza – you need to call someone thirty or forty times for the call to go through. I kept trying until I reached his family, made sure they were fine, and told him.

A woman I know got a scholarship to study in the US. She shared a heartbreaking post about how her mother would calm her down, saying it's not bad, even though the news reports and everybody she knows say the area is under heavy bombing.

4 p.m. It is no surprise that every family has lost at least one family member or someone they know. The unusual thing would be for a person to have not lost someone close. On WhatsApp, the best platform to communicate when the internet connection is low, I receive messages about a colleague who has lost her nephew; another who has lost a cousin; and a friend whose brother lost his wife.

The auto-complete feature on a mobile brings up potential words based on what you usually write. Now, there is no need to write a condolences message; all I do is type the first word and then start clicking on the following ones that show up to finish the message.

7 p.m. The whole family join us in the room we are staying in. We are talking, then the middle son, who accompanied me out earlier, says: 'I understand that many shops were opened to sell bread and basic needs. But can you imagine that the flower shop was open!'

Everyone smiles. But I think how wonderful it would be if someone gave me a bouquet of flowers. Pink and velvet roses . . . or, even better, tulips! That would be amazing.

Tuesday 17 October

8 a.m. I hear sounds outside the living room we are sleeping in. I can tell that someone is teaching the kids.

When the grandmother comes to see if we slept well, she tells us she dedicates an hour a day to teaching her grandchildren. 'It doesn't matter what I teach them, as long as they are learning something new. We shouldn't lose hope, and these kids are the future.' The oldest grandchild, Radwa, joins us. I ask what she learned today. 'I'm learning the multiplications table. The table of eight is the most difficult one.'

Ahmad, the middle brother, comes to say hi. It's clear he hasn't slept well. We know that he and his older brother take shifts during the night. 'We need to ensure that if something bad happens, one of us is awake and capable of saving the children at least,' he says.

In general, I'm a positive person, but during these times, Ahmad's optimism annoys me. If his predictions had been true, the escalation would have been over days ago. Every day, he comes and says it will end soon. We all give him a look of disbelief. We disagree with him because the reality around us shows no signs of solutions. The situation is vague, scary, and nothing is guaranteed.

10 a.m. 'We're about to run out of cooking gas,' the grandmother announces. Her son searches for available gas canisters but can't find any. The family is worried – they need to cook, to boil water to prepare the children's milk and sometimes to clean themselves.

55

I tell them we have an extra gas canister at my home in Gaza City. But who will go and get it? I call every person and taxi driver I know. No one is available . . . until the janitor of our building tells me that his family fled to the same area we fled to. He offers to bring the gas canister with him on his way to visit them, and I offer to pay for the taxi.

I understand that taxi drivers are jeopardising their lives, but the price the driver asked is insane! It's eight times the regular price of a private taxi. I start screaming over the phone, then I manage to lower the price to four times the regular one. I tell myself this is the only option. We need the gas.

Noon The grandmother comes to ask us what to prepare for lunch. The family feels guilty that since we fled to their home, days ago, we've barely eaten. In Gaza, even in the darkest of times, if you visit someone's home, they have to feed you and be good hosts. She gives us two options.

I look at her, smile and tell her: 'Both are fine. Anyway, what we don't eat today, we will eat tomorrow. It is not as if we are leaving any time soon. This dangerous situation is not coming to an end.'

2 p.m. We organise our bags for the tenth time. Every now and then we get things out to use or wear, and it becomes difficult to put them back in an organised way. We always ensure which bags are the top priority and which ones to leave behind, if we have to.

My sister gives me her wallet to put in one of the bags, then asks me to give it back to her. She takes her passport and says:

'Let me keep my passport with me. You never know, it might be needed to identify me in case something bad happens.'

4 p.m. I remember the driver who brought us from Gaza when we fled for the third time. I appreciate how calm he was on seeing how terrified, angry and lost my sister and I were. While driving, he received a call and started discussing what seemed like an important topic. Usually, I would have asked a driver to pull the car over until he finished the call or to let me out. But in that case, I did nothing.

When he finished, he told me that he's responsible for driving two daughters of a divorced couple. The couple don't communicate at all, and the driver is the mediator between them, even if the issue isn't related to the girls' commute. The woman decided to flee, but the man did not, and he had the children. She had called the driver to convince her husband to take the girls to her. The driver told her that he couldn't interfere in such a critical matter. He said that he felt sorry for the mother and her suffering. I felt sorry for the girls.

6 p.m. A friend of mine, who fled with his family from Gaza City, tells me about his neighbour, who stayed and is now hosting about seventeen cats. Four of them are house pets whose owners left them with the man, and the others are street cats that, after the destruction, found no food – and no one to feed them. Once the man fed one stray cat, the rest of her 'friends' joined – and now he is responsible for all of them. My friend is worried, since this man is now thinking about fleeing. I hope the situation gets better and he doesn't leave. For the sake of him and his family, and also for that of the cats.

8 p.m. I'm trying to sleep. For some reason, I think of that famous interview question: where do you see yourself in five years? Right now, all I'm thinking about is what will happen to me within the next five minutes. I've no clear mind to think of anything – but one thing I am sure of is that if we make it alive out of here, we are never going to be the same again.

9.20 p.m. It was a rumour.

After four o'clock you see no one on the streets. Everyone stays in their home for safety. Unable to sleep, I lie on the couch, trying to think of things to calm me down, when I suddenly hear a lot of noises outside. I go to the other room to ask the family what is happening. Once I open the door, I hear someone say: 'Everyone is evacuating.'

I don't even ask the reason. I tell my sister, who is on the phone, that people are evacuating. Both of us panic; we can barely put the cats in the carriers and take the top-priority bags. In her fear, my sister throws her mobile on the floor, takes the cats, and we go downstairs.

On our way down, the children are crying. Everyone is telling them that it's OK and nothing is going to happen. But we are terrified. Once we reach the street, we see an enormous number of people. It's complete darkness, which makes the situation more terrifying. My sister looks at me and says: 'Where shall we go? There is no place left.'

Suddenly, we hear a young man, in his twenties, screaming

and asking people to go back to their homes. We go to him and find out that it is a rumour. No one has been asked to evacuate, but one family decided to evacuate at night because 'someone said something to someone'. When people saw them leaving, everyone around them started to leave. It was the snowball effect.

We are terrified to go back; we stay for ten minutes, until we see other people going back and decide to do the same. We go upstairs. Fadel is screaming: 'As if we have enough energy to deal with rumours. My children are terrified, all the children are terrified.'

Ahmad follows and tells us that the neighbour's son ran down the stairs so fast that he fell and broke his hand.

We have evacuated several times and have thought about every scenario, to be ready, but it seems our bodies are not capable of dealing with this mental stress any more. My sister is unable to stand up, and I am shaking. The children are crying, and the men are screaming in anger. After half an hour, the grandmother comes with cups of tea with sage to calm everyone down.

11.30 p.m. My sister and I are left alone in the room. She looks at me and asks: 'This time it was a rumour, what about next time? We have fled three times, every place is dangerous, death is all around us, nothing positive is happening. There are no places left to flee to. If it weren't a rumour and we were forced to evacuate . . .'

She pauses for a while, but I know the scary question she is about to ask: 'Where to?'

Wednesday 18 October

8 a.m. I have not lost hope, but I have never been as peaceful as I am now with the idea of death. I am not sure whether it is because of the cruelty we are facing or the feeling of helplessness we continuously have . . . or whether I am just exhausted.

I cannot imagine that while I am 'safe', there are children under the rubble, some dead and some alive, whose stories took a very wrong turn. Those children were supposed to be having fun at school, going to amusement parks, and at night hearing bedtime stories about love and kindness. I'm still alive, while mothers are losing their children every day, fathers are incapable of sheltering their own families, and young people watch their dreams fade. Apparently, I am lucky – my turn hasn't come yet.

Today, I'm writing my diary while humming a song by Fairuz, a famous Lebanese singer, the Édith Piaf of the Arab world. My sister looks at me, not believing that after all the crying, terror and fear we had hours ago, I'm singing.

The song says:

The air breezed upon us, from the road of the valley.
Oh breeze, for love's sake, take me to my homeland.
I'm scared, oh my heart, to grow up in this exile,
And my home wouldn't recognise me.
Oh God! I miss my home. I am hopeful, yet I am full of
*   despair.*

9 a.m. I sit with my sister to prepare the list of things we need. The main item is medicine. My sister wants a muscle relaxant because 'all my muscles are tightened due to the fear', she says. Also, she asks for an antibiotic since she is not feeling well.

During these tough times, people in Gaza don't have the luxury of getting sick. There are no doctors available and no hospitals. No matter how hard I try not to watch the news, the news reaches me. Besides the well-known tragedy, my friend shares with me news about hospitals losing all electricity; patients having no space, especially in the intensive-care units; lack of medical supplies and dialysis patients skipping sessions; death.

I think of my dead mother again and tell my sister that I am grateful she is not experiencing what we are going through. My mother was sick, and we would take her to hospitals for appointments. I imagine having to take her in this situation; she couldn't have handled it.

My heart breaks for the patients and their loved ones.

10 a.m. Yesterday, a friend of mine, who fled with her husband to the south, shared with me that she and her husband have decided to go back north. 'We are staying with family members, but we're more than thirty-five people. I'm not comfortable; my children are not comfortable. We have agreed to leave.'

However, this morning, and after spending about twenty-four hours in northern Gaza, she sends me an SMS, telling me they have decided to go back. 'The streets are empty. There is no electricity, no internet connection, and there is

61

only one family in the building who has come back. If something bad happens, there is no one around. I have agreed with my husband to go back.'

As for us, we remain with the host family, hoping to go back to Gaza City soon.

Noon Do cats have nightmares? One of the cats keeps flinching all the time when asleep. My sister thinks she is having a nightmare.

I have no doubts that pets are smart – they understand certain commands and communication. But are our cats aware that we are displaced? That we had to evacuate three times and are living in fear? I couldn't help but wonder how to explain to your pet that something bad, out of your hands, is happening, and it is significantly affecting both of you.

4 p.m. Ahmad, the middle son of the host family, joins us for a cup of coffee. He tells us about a man he saw who evacuated with his family. 'He is a rich man with an elite social status. I never imagined seeing him in that state. He was standing in the queue of the bakery, waiting to buy bread.

'He looked miserable. Even though he was able to find an apartment for his family, he is still suffering. He is sixty years old and has no young members in his family, so one day he has to wait for hours for bread, and the next he has to wait for hours to fill the water containers and take them to the apartment.'

Ahmad also shares that he's tired of offering condolences to people he knows. 'After all of this ends, I will prepare a long list of every friend who has lost someone and offer them condolences one by one.'

When people ask me how we are doing, I no longer tell them we are OK. I tell them we are still alive. I've reached a stage where I am alarmed by the simplest of actions. Even when I hear a table being dragged, I jump up in fear, thinking it's a bomb. On the other hand, I do my best to do the smallest of things to remain positive – such as a five-minute nap, washing my face, talking to a loved one or even eating a chocolate bar.

We are in survival mode, and everything counts.

9 p.m. The night has come, and a number of airstrikes have hit the area. When the first one happened, I ran with my sister to put the cats in the carriers. Usually, the cats would be running out of fear. But this time, one of the cats was still, like a solid object. I held it and put it in the carrier, and we waited by the door in case we needed to leave.

My friend sends me a message saying there are airstrikes in her area, too. We write to each other about how tired, terrified and powerless we are. The same scenario every night, with few different details.

11 p.m. The roller coaster of emotions is killing me. Every day we go through mundane moments: happiness when something simple is achieved, such as buying bread or charging your phone, then fear and desperation after bombings and airstrikes. It is very difficult to process, very difficult to tolerate.

I think about what my gravestone would say if I died during this horrendous period. I find it impossible to come up with a statement – I don't even know what I want to achieve, what I want to say. I lay my body on the couch in the living room and close my eyes. Then, suddenly, I remember a poem I read one day and loved – I even kept it in my Notes app on my phone:

Do not stand at my grave and weep,
I am not there. I do not sleep.
I am a thousand winds that blow.
I am the diamond glints on snow.
I am the sunlight on ripened grain.
I am the gentle autumn rain.

. . .

Do not stand at my grave and cry,
I am not there. I did not die.

Thursday 19 October

8 a.m. I managed to sleep for four hours. It has been a long time since I achieved that. My friends, who always send me messages in the morning to check if I am still alive or, in their own words, 'just to see how you are doing', were happy to hear the great news.

I tried to wake up but couldn't. I felt as if I had no bones left; my body was soft and floppy. Every time I tried to raise my head up, it would sink back into the pillow. I felt like a big bowl of Jell-O.

Speaking of Jell-O, I really miss sweets. I have been trying to stay healthy and cut down on sugar, but if I get out of this, I will definitely give myself a sweet-treat day. I will eat vanilla and dark-chocolate ice cream; I love the combination between sweet and bitter. Also, I would love to eat *knafeh*, a traditional Arab sweet made with spun pastry, filled with cheese and soaked with syrup. In Gaza, we are special: we have our own version, filled with nutmeg, nuts and cinnamon instead of cheese. I could eat a ton of it right now!

10 a.m. The children, along with their cousin, decide to pay us a visit in the room. The youngest, Laila, brings me her notebook to show me the letters of the alphabet she is practising. At the beginning of each section, her grandmother has drawn a big version of the letter for her to colour in. She made me go through all the pages and was very proud.

While sharing their stories, one of them brings up the topic of a man with a hearing disability. I tell them a disability

65

is not about your body not being able to perform a certain function, but about not providing the means for the people to have a normal life.

I wonder how people with a disability are coping during these terrible times. With the lack of electricity and light, how will a person with a hearing disability be able to use sign language? What if they were separated from their family and found themselves in one of the shelters (if they are lucky) – do they know where to get water and what services are available? Is there a sign-language interpreter there?

What about those with a physical disability? Can they easily move, or even evacuate, with no lifts or ramps? Gaza was not designed to meet the needs of people with disabilities in the first place, but now it is much worse. It saddens me that even in miserable times, some people have better access and support than others.

Noon My wonderful friend who is living abroad sends me a message, saying that her Christian mother has activated 'a prayer army' for me, my sister and our loved ones, and we are protected in her bubble. I thank her very much and ask her to include our cats in the bubble, too.

As a Muslim, I'm blessed to have Christian friends among my close circle. We are always there for each other in good and bad times. They include me in their weddings and children's baptisms. Right now, the churches of Gaza are hosting Muslim and Christian families.

I have always believed in the power of prayer, no matter

what your religion or beliefs. Even for my atheist friends, I ask them to send me positive thoughts. I believe that love, in all its shapes and forms, is capable of changing this world and making it a much better place.

2 p.m. I go with Ahmad to get some stuff for the house. On our way, we see a boy of about fourteen, walking with what seem like his two younger sisters. They are holding bags of crisps in their hands, unopened. In a teasing manner, he tells them: 'Eat your crisps before we get bombed and die.' His words hit me hard.

Later, the grandmother, who was out of the house almost all day, joined us for coffee. She had been visiting her own family to help prepare bread with them, as many people had sought refuge in their home. She told us about how her oldest grandchild, Radwa, reacted to the escalation: 'In the first couple of days she stopped eating, and she rarely spoke. We were terrified. Now she is still scared, but at least she interacts with others and eats well.'

How many years of psychosocial support will be required to help these children process the many traumas they have been through?

6 p.m. From the window I see a bird land on a nearby tree. In my house, my sister has plants on the balcony where birds come for shade and food. She spreads bird food for them. The first time we evacuated, my sister was relieved that she had just watered the plants. She worried about them all the time. A few days ago, late at night, it rained, and my sister was glad. She told me that the rainwater washed the plants, they were taken care of.

I thought of the bird who chose this land, when it has the whole world to pick from. I wish I were a bird with no borders or limits, spreading my wings and living my life to the max, loving and feeling loved . . . I wish.

10 p.m. The grandmother opens the door without knocking. I was lying on the couch, but got up with a start.

'I am sorry,' she said. 'A church was bombed, and you told me you have friends there.'

We immediately checked and knew which church. My friend has been staying there with his family. I call him immediately . . .

'Are you OK?' I scream.

'No, I am not. They bombed the church.'

'I heard the fucking news! Are your wife and daughter fine?'

'They are. My parents are fine, too. They did not bomb the side we were in. But there are people under the rubble. We are trying to get them out. I gotta go. Tell our friends I am OK.'

In Gaza, no place is safe, not even churches.

Friday 20 October

8 a.m. I never thought that I, in my thirties, would become like one of those old people who wake up and check the newspaper obituaries to see who has died. In my case, it is the internet, not the newspaper – if we have a connection – and I check to see if anyone I know has died in the airstrikes and bombing. As for the age, I believe that you are as old as you feel, and these days I feel old. Very old.

A whole family I know have died. We were not close, but it is completely different when you match faces to the names, when you remember interactions. These were people of flesh, blood and memories who no longer exist. The idea of being alive one minute and then dead the next terrifies me.

Yesterday, the church in Gaza where many Muslim and Christian families were taking shelter was bombed. I know that my friend, his wife and daughter are fine. I call today to check on him. 'Until now, we are still getting people out from under the rubble,' he says. 'A relative of mine is dead and another one is in a critical condition in the hospital.'

He says they are in no state to think about future steps. I feel helpless. I wish I could be there for him.

10 a.m. Ahmad is a very helpful person. He is always working to help the families who evacuated with finding a place to stay; providing some basic necessities, like clothes, shoes and milk; or guiding them to where certain services are located.

Over a cup of coffee, he shares the tremendous impact of the situation on Gazans' livelihoods: 'A friend of mine had finally got a good income working as an online freelance pro-grammer. For the last two weeks, he hasn't done any work. He called me and said that he was out of money.'

For many Gazans, freelancing has been the 'ticket' out of unemployment. For the first time, Gazans did not need to cross a border or have a certain passport to be accepted; all they needed was a laptop, internet connection and electricity, and now even those are gone.

I wonder about the daily workers: the plumbers, the cleaners, the carpenters. How have they been able to afford these horrible times? Because disasters come at a price. How can they buy all their necessities with no income? I think about the young entrepreneurs I know, who started small businesses out of a talent they have or a gap they have filled in the market. Now that most of their shops are destroyed or damaged, I worry about their future.

Noon I want to stand up and scream.

This is the second Friday since the whole situation started. Fridays are when families gather for lunch, friends go out for fun, and people relax. For us, we are trapped, full of fear, waiting for the unknown.

It kills me to see on the internet pictures of long queues of people waiting to buy the iPhone 15, while Gazans are waiting in long queues to get bread and water for their families. I hate that many people around the world are not aware that we exist, and we are dying every day. I want to cry . . . and I desperately need a hug.

6 p.m. Since yesterday, the host family has been trying to secure drinking water. The water we have might last for a day or two. So far, they haven't succeeded, but they assure me there is nothing to worry about. I am worried.

My sister decides to reduce the amount of food and treats she gives the cats. Their food and stuff occupied the biggest space in the bags we took, but she says we are not sure how long this situation will go on, and we need to keep as much as possible.

The cats start meowing and going to the bag, trying to fetch a treat. At first, she refuses to give them anything, but then she caves in and gives them the treats.

10 p.m. I lie on the couch to count my blessings for the day. I remember that my cat jumped over my belly and started purring; Ahmad told me that a shop owner is selling products at lower prices for those who evacuated, because he wants to help; I saw a short video of Gazan children swimming in the sea; and – oh, I am still alive.

Saturday 21 October

8 a.m. The explosion this morning was so hard that I literally felt my body rise above the couch I was lying on.

The targeted house was metres away. I woke up, terrified, trying to get the cats with my sister, but this time I couldn't. There was such a loud buzzing and ringing in my ears that I couldn't focus. I couldn't balance either.

My sister got the cats, and we sat on the couches, as usual, waiting for a cue to move. Minutes later, she opened the door of the balcony. We couldn't see anything for dust. Later, Ahmad went to check and see what was happening. Ahmad – enthusiastic, positive Ahmad – came back, covering his body with his own hands, as if he was trying to hug himself. He looked lost . . . he was scared.

How long will this nightmare go on? How long?

9 a.m. Most of the windows of the host family's house are broken due to the bombing. When I open the toilet door, I realise that the medium-sized window there has fallen out, leaving a huge rectangular area of light and showing the window of the neighbouring building. I go backwards and return. The grandfather says: 'Go inside and do your thing. I promise you nobody will look.' I politely decline, saying I will wait until it is covered.

There are many new things I have forced myself to get accustomed to since this whole horrible situation started, but relieving myself in an open area where people can watch is not one of them.

Noon I get the chance to talk to my friend to check on her after five days of failed attempts. She tells me that she, who evacuated her house and is living in fear with her children, has volunteered to check on all her colleagues to provide them with emotional support. I can't believe her. Is she capable of absorbing all the negative energy of the others, is she fully equipped with what it takes to make them feel stronger? I wonder, in Gaza, who is helping the helpers, those who are trying to make a small, positive change?

I also receive a message from a friend abroad, telling me that she is amazed by my resilience and what a strong person I am. Who has told her that? Doing your best to survive is not resilience. I love and want to live life to the maximum. I want to travel, listen to music, learn new cultures. I don't want to be running for my own life. I don't want to pray every day that I live to see the sun of the next one. I am not resilient. I am weak, I am vulnerable. But I want to live.

In Gaza, for some, it is taboo to seek psychosocial support; people would rather live in shame instead of speaking openly about their problems. And for others, they are so consumed with providing the necessities to their families that they cannot even consider taking care of themselves. I believe every single Gazan is in dire need of therapy.

4 p.m. For the first time since we evacuated to this home, the grandmother has not prepared lunch. 'I am very sorry,' she says. 'For some reason, I can't cook today.'

But everyone knows the reason: this strong woman, who has been doing her best to keep her family and guests strong

73

during these tough times, is afraid. She sees death around her and finds herself helpless in its face.

6 p.m. We are still low on drinking water. After many attempts, they have only been able to fill five bottles.

They give me and my sister one, but we give it back. We still have two bottles with us, and they will benefit more from it. I am worried soon there will be no drinking water.

8 p.m. Sitting on the couch, focusing on nothing, hearing bombs from time to time, my sister and Ahmad start a conversation about theatre. They talk about the history of theatre in the Arab world and about the most iconic plays that have left an impact on the culture and public perspectives. They share their recommendations of their favourite plays.

I admire how they enjoy a normal discussion that any two people around the world might have.

I think back to a conversation I had earlier today with one of the kids. She asked me: if I could have a superpower, which one would it be? I told her that I would like to be invisible. I have changed my mind – I want the superpower of being normal, living a mundane life and discussing everyday topics.

Sunday 22 October

8 a.m. We don't have drinking water. Up until last night, the host family were telling us they were looking for alternatives. This morning, I realise that the five bottles they had last night are empty. They are asking for one of the two we still have.

I hear the grandfather talking to the water provider. Hearing the tone he uses, I would say he was a parent on his deathbed, begging his son overseas to come home and see him one last time. The water provider promises him he will come tomorrow or the day after.

I get really worried and start looking for solutions. I contact all the drivers I know in Gaza to see if anyone is willing to get us some water. Also, we need food for the cats.

If someone had told me that one day I would pay for water and cat food (and their delivery) the same price you pay for a piece of gold jewellery, I wouldn't have believed them.

We get water, we have cat food. We are fine for now.

10 a.m. We smell something burning. We find out that the woman living downstairs is burning wood to boil some water to clean her children.

When it comes to hygiene, I think of those staying in schools and hospitals for shelter. A normal person needs to wash their face, brush their teeth and run water over their body once a day. How many days has it been since those children washed themselves? And what about women? Do they have sanitary pads in case they get their periods? Even if there is water, is there enough privacy?

My sister's friend, who is staying with her family in one of the schools, told her that her diabetic mother is suffering. She needs to go to the toilet a lot because of diabetes. They talked to a family living next to the school and got their permission to let her mother go to them when she needs to. 'It is humiliating,' she tells my sister.

I check my phone and see a task I assigned myself a month ago – visit the doctor for a follow-up. I am still standing, but my health is deteriorating. I have this constant feeling of fatigue that refuses to let go of me. I am doing my best to continue taking my medicine on time.

Noon I need a tailor. One pair of shorts I have has a tear in the crotch; the zipper of the pocket of the other one is broken. I need the zipper to keep my wallet inside, so if we need to run at night, I won't be worried about it falling out.

I go with Ahmad to two tailors, but both shops are closed. We ask a man if anyone is available, and he points towards a small shop where the doors are slightly ajar. There, we find the woman who runs the place. She isn't here to work; she has no water at her home, so she and her children have brought the family's dirty clothes to wash them here. I can see a big bucket with the clothes in water and foam.

When we ask if she can help, she is hesitant, especially since her glasses are broken. 'I am not sure I can do a good job without my glasses,' she says. I tell her that right now, all I need is to wear shorts without a tear in the crotch. She starts doing the work patiently. At some point, she looks for thread that matches the colour of the shorts. I tell her I don't care, any colour will do.

She finishes the first pair and is working on the second pair when a huge explosion takes place. The children start crying, and we are terrified. I take the shorts and tell her it is OK, one pair is enough. I offer to pay her, but she firmly refuses. She prays for Ahmad and me to arrive home safely. Ahmad is so terrified that he can't even walk. We wait for a couple of minutes, until I send a message to my sister telling her we are alive. We move on.

6 p.m. I am terrified, not because of what is happening around us, but because I am getting used to it. My lost appetite is coming back to me. Now, under the bombing, I think about what we will have for lunch.

I am thinking about what to do tomorrow and the day after tomorrow and after a week, considering my current situation to be the only situation there is. I am used to the lack of privacy, the lack of high hygiene standards, the lack of movement and the lack of feeling safe.

What is going on? Is the abnormal becoming the normal? Is that all it takes? Two weeks of misery, and I start getting used to it? It is like getting used to living in darkness and forgetting about all the other colours. Can't I think of one colour to look forward to seeing?

9 p.m. My sister tells me that in the morning, she saw a tiny bird standing at the window. It was white with an orange beak. I tell myself this is a sign . . . I don't like orange, but orange it is. *Think of the colour orange . . . Think of the colour orange.*

Tuesday 24 October

8 a.m. I need to use the toilet. I can't wait.

Since we were evacuated to the third family's house, they have given us a small room to stay in, and the whole family sleeps in the wide hallway because, according to them, it is safer. If I want to use the toilet, I need to pass them, and they are sleeping, including the women. So I prefer to wait until they are awake. It is not that easy, and it makes me think about those who have to wait for hours in shelters and schools to reach a toilet that is probably filthy.

I go back to the room, and the cat does something funny. I laugh, then I cover my mouth with my hands, feeling ashamed. How am I laughing, when hours ago we woke up terrified after an airstrike hit the area? How am I laughing while, every day, hundreds of people are dying? I really hope no one heard me.

9 a.m. I meet Deya, an eleven-year-old neighbour of the family. He has green eyes and the most beautiful dimples you could see. Three days ago, Deya lost his cousin. I try to ask him how he feels about losing him. I expect him to cry or show sadness, but instead he starts telling me about his cousin: 'He is . . . I mean, he was the best football player among all of us. He would score all the goals, no matter how big the goalkeeper was. We both support Real Madrid. He told me that when he grows up, he wants to be a professional football player.'

I listen to him in fascination, not sure whether he does not realise what death is or whether he is denying it. We talk about other topics, like his favourite food and favourite colour. On his way out, I stress that it is OK to cry, especially as he lost a dear person. He looks at me and says, in a calm manner: 'I cannot imagine that he is no longer with us . . . I cannot believe that if I call him no one will answer.'

Noon I continue reading the book I found at the host family's house. This is the second book I've read here. For some reason, I tell myself that when I finish reading it, the whole situation will be over and we will go back to our homes.

One quote in the book says: 'We need to believe the lies in order not to die.' Is this what is going on with me? Am I lying to myself when I think that tomorrow will be better and the whole situation will end soon?

1 p.m. A neighbour from my original building sends a message to the building's WhatsApp group, saying that they don't have any bread, and he is begging all of us if we can get him and his family some bread.

3.30 p.m. I find a lizard in the room.

I go to the family members who are hosting us, protecting us from going through the misery of staying at schools, offering us food and taking care of us, and say: 'There is a lizard in the room. Unless it goes, I don't think I can stay here any more.'

'Don't worry, we will take care of it.'

'Please, don't kill it. Just get it out of the room, peacefully.'

'Any other orders?'

'No, thank you.'

6 p.m. Our cats are not OK. They are used to our – their – home. They know where everything is, and they feel safe there. Since we were evacuated the first time, they have been uncomfortable, and their actions reflect how confused they are.

While using a plastic tray as a fan, I notice that my sister is moving things around the room. She has decided to 'build a fort' for the cats. She gathers the cushions together and covers them with a blanket. The cats, who rarely sit next to each other, jump under the fort and remain silent. I am not sure whether the cats feel safer or not, but I am sure that my sister feels that she is doing her best to protect them and feels less guilty about all the suffering they have been through.

9 p.m. I finish reading the book, but nothing has happened. We are still away from our homes and we are not safe.

10 p.m. When the whole situation started, I made a decision not to write. But then a man whom I consider a mentor encouraged me to do so. I am grateful that I did.

During this period, writing has been my therapy, reflecting on the ongoing crazy events, taking a moment to absorb what is going on and putting things into perspective. With time, it has become my own shelter, the secret friend with whom I can't wait to share the chaos of my heart, soul and mind.

But I haven't had the energy to write lately. I just decided not to. I did not write anything yesterday, and was not planning to do it today. However, I found myself, late at night, writing.

Writing means that I am trying my best to survive. It means that I have hope that one day I will look back at these diaries and think of how long I have gone on. Because writing means that my heart is still beating . . . and my voice deserves to be heard.

Wednesday 25 October

8 a.m. Eighteen days have passed. We are still alive, but we haven't survived yet.

Ahmad comes to our room and asks if my sister and I would like something specific for lunch. My sister says she doesn't think she can eat. For the past five days, she has eaten almost nothing. I tell him that anything will be OK, and I thank his mother for her delicious cooking.

'So, you think my mother should open a restaurant?'

'Of course,' I say. 'But not here in Gaza, all the people have the same style of cooking.'

'I am not talking about here in Gaza,' he says. 'If we become refugees in another place again, she can open the restaurant there.' He winks at me.

Even though he is joking, his words send a chill down my spine.

9 a.m. I go with Ahmad to buy some necessities. I deliberately walk in the middle of the street so that, in case of a bombing, I will be – relatively – away from the buildings. I find myself humming a Taylor Swift song, 'Shake It Off'.

I see a girl, about ten, holding a gallon drum of water. She walks for two steps and then stops to rest, and so on. It is very clear it is too heavy for her. We are in such a hurry that we do not stop and offer help. In these days, everyone tries to run their errands as fast as possible and get home before something bad happens. I feel ashamed.

I reach the pharmacy, and I'm shocked. Due to a nearby

airstrike, all the glass doors are broken. The pharmacy has turned into an open market, yet they are still working.

An old man comes in and asks about his medicine. The pharmacist apologises and tells him that there are no alternatives either. 'I still have seven pills left,' the man says. The pharmacist looks at him sympathetically and answers: 'Hopefully the whole situation will end soon, and you will be able to get your medicine again.'

9.30 a.m. In another shop, I hear a man talking over the phone, saying he can't host any new people. 'There is no space left. I have my sisters and their families, and two of my cousins with their families. The men are sleeping in the street so the women can have a place to sleep upstairs.'

The man also speaks about the scarcity of water. He has even calculated how much water goes with every toilet flush.

I also notice the variety of accents I am hearing. It's like all areas of Gaza are in the same place. Actually, all the areas of Gaza *are* in the same place. Gaza is a densely populated area, and now half of it has evacuated to the next half. Double the number, half the space.

10 a.m. We go to a third shop, and I hear the owner describing a 'hot chick from Gaza City' he saw this morning. I feel sick. I have always been against objectifying women, but I cannot imagine what women and girls who have left their homes feel when buying necessities for their families while someone is checking them out. It is just disgusting. On the

84

other hand, it is very rare. Every man I meet, except for this individual, has been respectful towards women during these times.

Ahmad tells me he has to go to a friend who is staying in one of the schools. 'He called me, crying. He evacuated with his family, and now they have no money. I need to go and give him some money and bring him some food.'

Ahmad leaves quickly to help the man and his family. I admire this young man. He and his family are going through the same misery as the rest of us, yet they are hosting us and helping others as much as they can.

3 p.m. My friend sends me a text to check on me. We were supposed to have lunch, days before the whole situation started. She had to cancel, however, and promised me we would meet the next week.

'When all of this is over, we should go and have that lunch we agreed on,' I write. 'See, this is what happens when you cancel your plans.'

'We will have two lunches and three dinners,' she replies. 'I just hope this horrible nightmare will be over.'

After some minutes, she sends another message: 'I really miss you.'

'Listen, I don't want to start crying now,' I say. 'It will be over, it will be over.'

'I want to cry, too,' she says. 'But I cannot cry in front of my children, and there is no place where I can cry alone without anyone hearing or seeing me.'

5 p.m. I am sitting in my room. The children and the neighbour's children are playing. At first, the neighbour's children never visited out of fear, but now they come almost every day. I hear them having a 'make-believe birthday party'.

It is easy to decide whose birthday it is, and what age, but the toughest conversation is about the cake. After long deliberations, they agree it is going to be a chocolate cake. Very big – five layers – stuffed with chocolate, with figures of superheroes and princesses – made of chocolate as well, of course – on top.

I can't help but smile and wish I could be playing with them so as to convince them to have a vanilla cake instead . . . or maybe an orange cake.

7 p.m. Lying on the couch, I think about how silly it would be if I died one day before it was over.

In an attempt to get rid of such negative ideas, I go back to humming Taylor Swift's song.

Thursday 26 October

11 a.m. Ahmad and I are going back to his home after buying medicine and food, when we see a group of cats in the land next to where he lives. Ahmad goes back to the shop and buys some mortadella to feed them.

All the cats are standing at a distance. When Ahmad throws the pieces, they come, pick them up and run away. However, one cat approaches us and is friendly, but the closer she comes, the more shocked we become. The cat has lost an eye, has been bitten all over her ears and has marks across her body. It's clear she's a house pet that has been abandoned.

Ahmad's nephew and two nieces see us, so they come down and start helping feed the cats. Apparently, they've assigned each one of the cats a funny name. This one they've called Manara, which means 'lighthouse'. They tell me that she appeared only a few days ago, which makes me think that the owners have left in a hurry, or maybe their house was bombed. We play with it for a while and then go home.

I tell my sister what happened, and we ask around to see if someone can help, but in these times, nobody can. We agree to take care of the cat by giving it food, morning and night. I'm not satisfied, though, and suggest we keep it with us until we can find a safe place. My sister says that's hard, as we are staying in one room, in someone else's house, and are not sure what the future holds, plus we already have two cats who are our priority, and we just cannot take an extra one. I can't disagree with her because everything she says is right.

4 p.m. I'm trying to sleep, especially as I couldn't sleep at all during the night due to the bombing. I hear a knock on the door, and the grandmother comes in. She says: 'You have a guest.'

Reaching the house we are in is not that easy. You need to take some stairs up, then turn a couple of times and go up to the first floor.

I stand up and go to the door, and see Manara the cat. I can't believe it. Did she follow us? No way, we saw her hours ago. I go to the room and ask my sister, who is on the phone, to end the call and come.

When my sister comes out and sees the cat, she covers her mouth with her hands and starts to cry. I look at her and say: 'If this isn't a sign, I don't know what is.'

We agree, standing there at the door, to take the cat in and keep it with us until the situation is over, and until we find her a safe place and good people to take care of her. We give her food, my sister tries to clean her, and we watch her sleep.

My sister tries reaching any vets in the area. Since we don't live here, we don't know anyone. After many calls, she's able to reach someone. He promises to try to check on the cat. Hopefully, things will go well.

I look at my sister and say: 'This cat is sent to us from God. Now, I am relieved.'

'What do you mean?' she asks.

'I mean, maybe this cat is the mercy we receive to get us out of this whole situation. And even if we die, we will die on a good note . . . having done something good.'

7 p.m. Today has been horrible. We hear the news about more areas evacuating. There is uncertainty all over the place. Everyone is suffering because of the lack of electricity and water. The fear is increasing. Bad news everywhere.

But, deep inside, today I felt good because we've been adopted by Manara, our lighthouse.

Friday 27 October

4 a.m. It was another hard night. I, my sister and the two cats were not able to sleep. Manara, the abandoned cat we took in, was sleeping peacefully. I don't think the words 'tired' or 'exhausted' would describe her state. The word that came to mind is one I heard in an old Arabic song; it could be translated into 'crushed by exhaustion'. It is weird how the cat found safety among people who are in dire need of a safe haven; she came to us while we are away from our home, the place we belong to.

A few nights ago, we started a new tradition, since it seems the situation is going to last for a long time. The guys of the house started playing cards, joined by their cousin. Most of the time I will let them play and will just watch while reading a book or writing my diaries.

The cousin is in the last year of high school, the 'definitive year', according to us, because this year's marks determine which faculty you can join. While playing, the cousin started talking about how the students had studied for one month only before the situation started; he worries about what will happen to him and the thousands of students. There are many challenges. The clearest one is that people who lost their homes are staying in the schools. Where will they go? They have no homes left.

Also, can the students, who are traumatised and most probably have lost someone close, be able to learn? And what about the teachers, the heroes who not only teach, but also build students' characters? Do they have enough energy to do their noble work? Studying is your way to a better future. I doubt our students see any future after what has happened.

10 a.m. My sister took the cats, including Manara, to the vet. He agreed to open his clinic for half an hour.

The road was not safe, but my sister was ready to take the risk – 'It is for the cats!' The taxi drivers, who used to make lots of money, stopped working when the fuel ran out. Ahmad went out into the street and started asking the neighbours, and finally he found one. He was a wonderful man who did not charge her a lot.

My sister told me that the vet's hands were shaking after a miserable night. He wanted to give one of the cats a pill. In these situations, the cats resist, so together my sister and the vet were supposed to hold her to give her the pill. The doctor stopped after the second try and asked her to crush it and put it in the food. 'He wanted to cry,' my sister told me. Manara has a lot of inflammation in the mouth and stomach. He gave her an antibiotic shot and said she still needed to take two more, but he was not planning to open the clinic again. 'Figure it out,' he told my sister.

Noon On my way to get some basic needs, I witnessed a new way of getting water. People were using a pulley. They would fill a big tank of water in the street and then fill buckets of water and take them up to the roof using a pulley. It would take hours, but they were doing it gladly.

After a long search, we were able to find an additional small battery to buy. We connected it to a small device into which you put the charger cord to charge the mobile. It can charge one at a time and takes several hours. I discuss with my sister, almost daily, how evacuating is like preparing for a new house – you need to buy a lot of things, and everything is expensive.

Today, I dropped my mobile for the hundredth time since the beginning of this week. I picked it up and talked to it. 'Listen,' I said. 'I don't have the luxury of losing you. I cannot even replace you, even if I have money. You are my only connection with this world during these horrible moments. So you need to promise me that you will stick with me at least till we get out of this. Deal?'

3 p.m. The grandmother paid us a visit. It is weird how in these situations, where death is behind every door, people are so traumatised that they speak of sad and happy events at the same time. She started by telling us about a woman she knows who has four sons. They all travelled abroad to work and send her money, so that she could build the family dream home for them to come back and settle down in.

'The whole building is gone. All their hard work for years has gone, just like this. The mother is devastated.'

After that story, she shared some of the wedding traditions of the family. There are up to seven nights of celebration for the women of the groom's family, led by his mother. Every day they wear something different. Every day there is a certain type of food: pastries, chicken dishes, Western cuisine, etc. During these celebrations, the women sing and dance till late in the night.

The guys also have festive times. One activity is called the *arghul* event. The *arghul* is a flute. The *arghul* player starts singing, and the guys dance and create the rhythm for him. This can take hours. For the *dehia* dance, the guys stand in two opposite lines and dance to the same rhythm while clapping their hands. After the party, they eat a traditional dish called *sumaqia*.

5 p.m. I wondered, while sitting with the guys playing cards, if one day I would go out into the streets and, instead of seeing evacuated people wearing torn clothes and looking for food and medicine, I would attend a wedding and see men dancing to the *arghul* and *dehia*, while women were in their own party, wearing embroidered dresses, singing and dancing.

6.30 p.m. I checked my phone and noticed that the signal bars of both SIMs were marked with an 'X'. I heard people outside the room talking about the loss of the signal. I thought of the worst-case scenario: have the communication companies stopped working in Gaza? Some people, including my sister, were sceptical about this, but an hour later, after checking the radio, it was verified. All communication channels have stopped working; we don't have access to the internet, not even via data. We cannot receive any messages and we cannot make any phone calls.

We were not afraid; we were terrified.

We never thought the situation could get worse. We have already been living in continuous fear and facing death every second. Now, there is more – we are blindfolded.

This means we cannot know what is going on around us, we cannot check on our loved ones in other areas of the Gaza Strip, we have no access to any emotional support of any kind and, scariest of all, if anything happens to us, no one will know.

If the past three weeks were scary, the coming ones will be brutally insane . . .

Saturday 28 October

6 a.m. I am sure that no one in the Gaza Strip slept at all. Since all the communications were cut, we were terrified to death. The waiting for something bad to happen while everybody is completely clueless was horrifying. We just heard the sounds of airstrikes, without knowing where they were.

I thought of every possible downside to what has happened. For instance, our friends and family members who live abroad and who are trying to contact us via the internet or through international calls suddenly find themselves unable to reach us.

What if someone gets injured and needs an ambulance to go to the hospital, which cannot even provide medical support? There are no phones to call. You will simply wait for a miracle to happen.

What is going on? Someone tell us something – anything.

8 a.m. After discussions, all night long, we reached the only idea that will calm us down. We simply cannot control anything. We need to take it one day, and night, at a time. We are disconnected from the whole world. We are clueless. Let's hope for something good to happen and pray nothing bad does.

We all knew that us reaching this 'belief' was our way of numbing the feelings of fear and terror, but for once we all chose to lie to ourselves, because without this, we will go crazy.

9 a.m. Manara the cat needs another shot of the medicine. The vet that helped us on Friday said he cannot help any more. There are no phones. Ahmad went into the street and started asking all the neighbours about any nearby vet. After an hour, he told us about a man who 'gives injections to animals, but he is not a vet, he is an animal lover'. The man has already evacuated with his family, but he visits his house every three or four days to put out food for the pigeons. Ahmad asked every neighbour to ask him to visit us so that he can give the cat the injection.

Noon My sister and Ahmad went to the pharmacy to get Manara an antibiotic for human babies, to give it to the cat as a precautionary move. They also went to bring back some food. After they left, there was no connection between us – if something bad happened to them, we wouldn't even know about it.

An hour passed, and I was at home, worried sick. I could hear the continuous airstrikes and hits, not knowing where they were happening. I could not even send an SMS to check on my sister. There was nothing I could do.

I started praying. I recalled all the prayers I knew. The cats were lying in the room, on separate couches. Then I decided to listen to music. I turned on a song I like and raised the volume up, not caring about what others outside would think, and sang along:

Maybe he forgot, because of all the pictures he deleted and the denial he is living in . . .

*Maybe he forgot that on his forehead, his whole story is
written . . .*

They arrived an hour later. Ahmad told me that within
two days, there will not be anything left in the shops. Many
items have already disappeared from the aisles.

1.30 p.m. My sister pulled an orange out of the bag. She
told me she wanted some fruit and had been able to get four
oranges and four apples. The orange looked damaged, and
my sister, who wouldn't have touched it in the past, was
cleaning and eating it quietly.

I looked at her and said: 'It seems the whole situation is
gonna last for a long time. We need to be patient.'

My sister replied: 'I have no patience left.'

2.30 p.m. Even though I am sure there is no connection at all
with the outer world, or even the local one, I couldn't stop
checking my mobile every five minutes to check the signal.
I even tried sending messages on WhatsApp and SMS, but
they never went through.

The only way of knowing what is going on is through the
radio or the TV. Only a few people with solar power and
TVs are able to watch the news. People walk to other streets
just to hear if there are any new updates.

Ahmad's brother told us he saw a man screaming in the
street. Some family members of his did not evacuate, and
on the news he heard that the area they were in had been
heavily targeted. He did not know if they were still alive or

dead; he just wanted answers, whether good or bad. People were trying to calm him down, but it did not work. 'He went crazy,' Ahmad's brother said.

10 p.m. To kill time, I played cards with the guys. They were talking about how, in over twenty days, they haven't earned any money. Another reason to be worried. I was almost absent-minded the whole time. I won the game!

11 p.m. If we die, when will people even notice we are gone? Will we be buried under rubble alive? Or die immediately?

Will anyone tell the world that I had many dreams? And that I wanted to visit Italy and Morocco one day? Will anyone tell my story? Or will I be 'a guy who died'?

Sunday 29 October

3.55 a.m. I am barely able to sleep. My body is aching. I cannot even determine which part is in more pain than the other. I am just exhausted.

'The connection is back! The connection is back!'

I hear these words coming from my sister, who is sleeping on the couch. In less than two seconds, I am up, my phone in hand, checking to see if what she says is correct. The connection really is back.

My adrenaline kicks in, and suddenly my sister and I – and the host family members outside – start sending messages and calling our loved ones.

'I thought I would never hear your voice again,' my friend tells me, crying. She says my call is the best one she has ever received in her whole life. I know she has received better ones, but I can imagine the fear she and all our loved ones must have felt.

Checking my WhatsApp, I find many messages starting with 'Even though I know you cannot read my message, I want to tell you that . . .', from many people. Some mention how much they love me, others how scared they are, and others speak of seeing me after the whole thing is over. I reply to all of them.

My other friend, even after talking over the phone, keeps sending me messages. We speak about how worried we are feeling. Then, at the end, I send her a message: 'Regardless of everything, I am extremely grateful that the connection is back. The situation hasn't changed, and our misery is on-going . . . but the connection is back!'

8 a.m. I can't go back to sleep. I go to the toilet. The door is open, yet I hear a sound coming from inside, saying it is occupied. It is one of the children. The grandmother tells me that since the situation started, the oldest grandchildren have been keeping the toilet door open, and the youngest won't go unless one of her parents, or her grandmother, is with her.

10 a.m. Manara the cat is slowly getting better. Unfortunately, we still don't have the chance to give her the injection she needs, but my sister is giving her an antibiotic intended for children. She is eating, her ears are clearing up, and she is sleeping a lot.

While she is cleaning Manara, my sister notices some new scars. The cat will meow loudly when she touches a certain part and, after checking it, we find another mark under the fur.

My sister is worried sick about Manara. She says that as well as all the medical care she requires, we also need something to strengthen the remaining eye. She bases this on her previous experience with another cat.

I try to be realistic: 'We are doing the best we can. We need to take it one day at a time.'

I wish Manara could tell us what her story is, who hurt her and how deep her suffering is.

11 a.m. I am with Ahmad, getting some vegetables and a torch, when I see one of my best friends walking in the street. He was the one who asked me to help him find a new place to stay, since his aunt's house is hosting more than seventy people, and there is no more space for anyone or anything. Unfortunately, I was not able to help him.

I am very happy to see him. I wave at him, and we hug. In the past, every time I saw my friend, I would compliment him on his nice outfits. This time, he looked very bad; his clothes were not matching and didn't fit his body. He was tired. He was not well.

I introduced him to Ahmad, saying that he is one of my best friends in the whole world, and introduced Ahmad to him as 'one of the people kind enough to host us'.

We speak for less than a minute. He says he is OK. I tell him I am OK. Both of us are not OK.

I leave him after we both say we will meet after this all ends and have a nice cup of tea by the sea. I keep walking, with tears in my eyes.

Later, I send him a message: 'I was so happy to see you. Seeing you was the best thing to happen to me today (well, the second best after getting the connection back). Until we meet again, my friend.'

3 p.m. Ahmad is reading stories to the children. He is sharing a story about a chicken that did something and then started singing. It is clear that the children have heard the story before, since they are contributing to it and singing with him.

Everyone in the host family begs Ahmad not to sing because he has a terrible singing voice. I tell him there are many amazing, good qualities about him. He is positive,

101

kind, and he helps everybody. Having a good singing voice is not one of those qualities.

8 p.m. For the hundredth time, I am repacking the bags to get everything in place in case we need to leave again. My sister points out that this time, I do not care about my laptop or other things I used to see as a priority.

10 p.m. My emotional ability to continue writing is strong, but my physical ability is not. When I was buying the torch this morning, I asked Ahmad if he thinks we will reach a stage where we go back to using candles, if we can find any.

Just like a candle, I feel that I am slowly fading . . . my body is losing its strength. I have no energy left.

I am writing, but everything I write is a drop in the ocean. Like Manara, I feel only a part of me is expressing the pain I am going through, yet there are many left voiceless. I wish I could let out every emotion and experience and thought I have. I wish the walls could talk to share the fear we're living in between them all night.

I wish the sky could talk to share everything it witnesses: people roaming the streets, not knowing where to go or whether they will have food for the next day – or whether they will be alive.

I wish the mirrors could talk to share the tragedy on our faces that is adding so many years to our actual age. I wish someone could hug me and tell me it is over.

Monday 30 October

10 a.m. 'I have made the most difficult decision of my life. I am leaving with my kids, without my husband.'

My friend told me this when we spoke about the scenarios for us in this unbearable situation. Her husband has a lot to take care of – his work and his extended family. But, for my friend, her children's safety comes first, even if this means leaving her husband behind. As she told me, she started crying.

The conversation about whether people should stay or leave, if it is even going to be their decision in the first place, is being held everywhere in Gaza. Some are ready to leave immediately, 'until it gets better'; some are not even considering the option, believing 'dying in my own place is better'; while some are torn. Will this pain ever come to an end?

Noon I hear the grandmother yelling at one of her sons. It turns out that a neighbour asked for drinking water, which is scarce, and the son decided not to give him any. She insists that he does. 'Anything you give others will get back to you. Don't worry, we were able to find drinking water before, and we can find it when this is over. We need to help each other in these difficult times.'

The grandmother is loved by everyone, old and young. I admire how hard she is trying to keep calm.

Later, I saw her dressed and going to visit a relative nearby. Since there are no doctors, she went there to perform the 'egg technique' on a newborn child. When a child is held in a certain way, their bones and ribs can start hurting. This is usually caused by something like a slightly dislocated bone. The grandmother takes the egg yolk and passes it over the body of the child. It becomes softer until it reaches the painful part, then it becomes liquid. This happens because of the higher temperature. She keeps the yolk on that part and covers it with gauze. After a couple of days, the pain is gone. 'I learned it from an old lady in the neighbourhood a long time ago, and it has always worked out,' she says.

3 p.m. To be honest, I am tired of talking about Gaza. Even those outside Gaza, they only speak about us. I want to talk about books, music, love, food and work. However, this is a privilege I cannot enjoy.

'I had to walk with my husband for about twenty minutes to reach someone we know who has bread,' a friend tells me. 'I am asking my children to eat half a loaf; my son is a teenager now, and he used to eat much more than half a loaf.'

I receive a WhatsApp message from a wonderful friend who lives abroad, sending a picture of the beautiful mountains near where she lives (the picture takes a lifetime to open) and telling me that one day she will take my picture there when we go together. And she promises lots of junk food, which I love. I react with 'love', yet my heart aches.

4 p.m. It is no longer a surprise when you hear of hundreds of people staying in one house because they have nowhere else to go. I heard today about a man I know who is staying with almost sixty people in a chalet. At night, some of them sleep in the cars or under the stairs to make space for others. They use the stagnant water in the pool for flushing the toilet. Sixty people, almost half of them children, living in these conditions . . .

6 p.m. Every time we open the door of the room we are living in, the young cat tries to escape. All of us run after her, until we get hold of her. I completely understand. For almost a month, she has been trapped in one small room, away from home, and she can feel the huge stress we are going through. Today, she escaped three times. Our big fear is if she escapes and we can't find her.

After the third time, my sister came into the room and started sobbing. 'I want to go to my home. I want safety. Is this too much to ask for? I cannot handle this any more. I cannot.' She spoke a lot, and I listened to her for a while. However, I had to be the voice of reason as well. I told her that this is going to take a long time. We need to be as patient as we can. It is not going to get easier any time soon.

8 p.m. I am able to load Facebook on my mobile (the internet is very poor). I see a few posts: two from people asking for an apartment or room to rent for those coming from the north of Gaza, and one from an elderly lady who has nowhere to go.

Some posts show pictures of men and women who have died. One is of a young guy who got married just before the whole situation started. The words of mourning break my heart.

There are posts asking for a place that sells food, and another from someone asking for a certain medicine that they are willing to pay any amount of money for.

I close the application.

10 p.m. On my mobile, I have a voice-activated 'personal assistant'. Sometimes I press on something by mistake and a screen appears, encouraging me to use this feature.

Today, the message was: 'Try saying, "Sing me a lullaby."'

Lying on the couch, I couldn't stop thinking about that message: 'Sing me a lullaby.' Do people know what 'lullaby' is being sung for the children of Gaza? Do they know the kinds of sounds they hear every night?

Do parents realise that while they are reading bedtime stories to their children, other parents, in a place called Gaza, are holding theirs close to their hearts and praying that nothing bad will happen?

I am thirty-five years old . . . and I miss my mother. I wish I could bury my face in her hands and listen to her singing me a lullaby.

Tuesday 31 October

8 a.m. Manara, the cat we took in, is getting better. My sister is taking great care of her. Judging by the marks on Manara's body, my sister thinks she was in a house that was destroyed. 'It feels like a number of heavy objects fell on her tiny body.'

While the big cat was not bothered, the small one was irritated by Manara. Every time she came near, she would hiss. Usually, when you bring a new cat home, you should keep it away from the others in a separate room until they get used to it. In our case, we are all in one small room, and we are not at home.

Manara, on the other hand, is very grateful for being with us. When my sister puts out food, she waits patiently. She eats anything offered to her. And when she's finished, she goes back to a box that was used to carry the sand that passes for cat litter. I think she chose this torn box to show that she does not want to bother anyone, she just wants to stay with us.

10 a.m. I go out to buy some items, but this time, I go by myself. I go to a shop, looking for a small bag. A lady comes in and asks for something. The shopkeeper tells her: 'It is not available. Once we sell out of a product these days, it is gone. We cannot bring in new ones.'

The lady looks upset and says something like: 'They left nothing.'

I find a small bag. I want to use it for the many chargers and leads we have accumulated. I ask about the price and am surprised by the number quoted. I am blessed that I can pay, but I have to say something.

'Your prices are really expensive. This is not fair,' I say.

'No, no, we have the best prices,' the shopkeeper says. 'Go and ask in the other shops and compare.'

'You know very well that nothing is left in the other shops. And we are in no state to keep walking and checking other places. Your prices are very expensive, and what you are doing is not good.'

I pay and leave.

11 a.m. I go to a shop that still has some food and other products. The shop size is medium, but the number of people who want to buy is huge. Two workers stand at its doors, allowing only a few people in every fifteen minutes.

Once I'm in, I start choosing what I need. I get pushed so hard that I have to stop and tell the guy behind me that there is a woman in front of me and he is pushing me into her.

Then I find treasure. Four tiny soda cans that are cold! I buy them and go directly to show them to my sister. It has been a long time since we drank something cold. Even though she does not drink soda, she takes one of the cans and drinks it like it's the most expensive drink in the world.

When Ahmad joins us, we talk about how every area had its own market day. Sellers would come from all over the Gaza Strip to sell their products. Now, there are no markets left.

4 p.m. I am talking to my sister, when she refers to an incident that happened before the situation started as 'in the good times'. I say we have never had any 'good times'. Even when things were relatively stable, Gazans suffered. We did not have a reliable electricity supply; we couldn't travel easily, and some could never travel at all; unemployment was very high and life was far from normal. It is just that we have bad circumstances and deadly ones. I might be exaggerating, but this is how I see things.

We also talk about how many things we have bought since we evacuated. I joke with my sister and say that all we need now is a carpenter to put up a couple of shelves in our room to give us more space.

My sister does not laugh.

8 p.m. The news is not good. The situation is getting worse – horrible and terrifying things are happening. The level of our fear is beyond normal. Nothing shows any sign of hope. I tell my friends that I am not sure we will see another morning.

10 p.m. I hear Ahmad outside, reciting a poem I love. I am not sure what prompted him, but hearing it warmed my heart:

When you prepare your breakfast, think upon others
Don't forget to feed the pigeons.
When you engage in your wars, think upon others
Don't forget those who demand peace.
And when you return home to your house, think upon others

Such as those who live in tents.
When you fall asleep counting planets, think upon others
Who cannot find a place to sleep in.

Is anyone thinking of us? And are we going to end up living in tents, or worse, become one of those who cannot find a place to sleep in?

Wednesday 1 November

5 a.m. We notice that the connection is cut for the second time. No phone calls, no text messages and no internet. Unlike the first time, I put my mobile down, close my eyes and try to have some minutes of sleep.

I am numb, completely numb. I am too tired of being afraid. I don't have more energy to be hopeful. My body is unable to react. I am losing my ability to feel.

8 a.m. I reread the messages I received last night. One of them shows a picture of a beautiful cat, with the text: 'This is a street cat that has chosen our house (or at least the garden) as his home. He is very shy. My wife named him Rubio, which means blond in Spanish. I am sure he somehow is connected to Manara.'

Speaking of Manara, she is still improving. Today, for the first time, she was playful for about ten minutes. She went around the room, cuddled with us and chased a fly, which I allowed. I have this rule: 'If a cat is being fed, it is not allowed to follow flies. Flies have the right to live.' But the fly was far away, so I did not stop Manara from chasing it. Another good sign is that the bloating of her lower abdomen has decreased significantly. I thought she was pregnant, but she isn't.

I thought of a friend of mine whom I tried to call yesterday but couldn't catch. When she returned my call, I saw her name on the mobile, but did not feel like answering. I was too tired. I decided to talk to her the next morning. For a second, I wondered whether I had lost my chance to ever hear my friend's voice again.

Noon The connection is back. I answer calls, reply to text messages and put my mobile down.

1 p.m. 'I am thinking about distributing my children among the different homes of relatives.'

'Why? To reduce the burden?' I ask.

'No, in case something bad happens, I would lose one of them, not all.'

That was the conversation I had with a man I know over the phone. I was asking him if he knew of any available gas canisters. I was in the middle of the street, trying to catch a better signal. I finished the call and sat down on the pavement. I wanted to cry, to scream, but I couldn't.

It is like one of those 'muted' videos. The amount of misery is reaching levels I have never thought it would . . . What else is left? What else?

3 p.m. A friend called, checking on us. She told me that her family decided to get a single solar panel, to be able to charge batteries and mobile phones. It cost them more than $600.

They were lucky to find one. In Gaza, $600 is the monthly salary of three people working twelve hours a day. This is how horrible the situation is. Even though the minimum wage is way higher, many young Gazans find themselves facing two options: accepting a job that does not require the university degree they hold, with a very low salary that can cover transport and a few necessities – or be jobless, without hope of a good life.

The sad thing about my friend's story is that, at the end of the day, not all the family members are satisfied. Some of them are not getting their items fully charged, especially when the sun is not that strong.

5 p.m. I realise that today is 1 November. My sister thinks nothing has changed, it is just a date. But, for me, everything has. It is almost a month since the whole situation started; if we make it through alive, no October will ever pass without pain in our hearts. October has marked the loss of many lives and memories – what will November hold?

8 p.m. I receive a call from my friend who has lost her home, checking on me. We belong to a group of friends, almost all in our mid-thirties, yet she has just turned thirty. She always brings joy to the group. During our conversation, she shares some fun situations that happened to her at the school she is staying at. I tell her that I cannot imagine how she is maintaining her positive attitude.

'This experience has taught me how to appreciate the smallest of things,' she says. 'Drinking clean water; having water to take a shower; eating a healthy meal that has vegetables and protein in it; sleeping for eight hours . . . Oh! I miss sleeping on my bed.' Then she says: 'Believe me, the real challenge is when the situation ends. Going back to reality and having to make decisions about every single part of your life. Right now, we are in the middle of chaos. But then, when the silence arrives, and you start seeing everything clearly, the real catastrophe will start.'

11 p.m. This morning, when I was able to sleep for a short while, I dreamed about two birds. They were both chained, and the female had something covering its beak. I approached them and took the chains off, unleashed the beak and set them free.

I am not sure whether this is a sign that something positive will happen soon or whether it is my subconscious trying to let out my feelings. One thing I am sure of is that I want to be free . . . free like a bird.

Thursday 2 November

9 a.m. There is no reason for me to go out, but I want to walk. Just walk.

Unless you need something important, you don't leave your place. But I can't handle it any more. I go to the street and start walking quickly. It is like I have this huge energy inside me. I go to new streets and areas. I don't care.

I reach a library. It is open. Some libraries have started selling random things since the situation started. The other day, I bought a hat from a library that was also selling pyjamas and underwear. I enter and buy a highlighter pen, for when I find quotes I like while reading. Since the beginning of October, I have read two books, and now I am reading a third.

After around an hour, I decide to go back. I see a lady coming towards me. I do not recognise her at first, but then I remember: I had been working with her. She had to evacuate south and stay with her in-laws. We exchange a few sentences and move on.

The irony is that we had been working together on an art project. A month ago, we were discussing expressing feelings via acting, singing and dancing. Now, we are two people, far away from home, unable to express their pain and constant fear.

How come we were thinking of a better future for Gaza and its youth then, when now we are not sure we will see another day?

How come this lady, who used to wear colourful clothes and have a smile that would light up a room, is a replica of herself, in a completely black outfit, with eyes full of sadness?

10 a.m. On my way back, I see a nurse coming out of a super-market, holding a bottle of juice in his hands. I know he is a nurse because he is wearing his uniform. I wonder about the horrible things that this man has been witnessing every single day. How tired he must be that he can't even change before leaving the hospital – or maybe he just took a break.

How can doctors and nurses be saving lives if their own families are in danger? How can they operate when there are hundreds more waiting for help? How can they have the clarity of mind to make decisions while hearing the bombing around them?

2 p.m. I receive a message from someone living abroad, tell-ing me that 'Your dignity is in my heart.' Even though I was touched by this message and others she sent out of support and care, I was a little bit sarcastic about it. My dignity? I have some?

In 'normal' times, Gazans don't have the dignified ability to travel whenever they want. I have been blessed to travel several times, though there were many chances I lost because I couldn't secure a travel permit. I would get selected for programmes out of thousands of people around the world, and get disqualified for not being able to travel.

The most horrendous one was when I was selected for a human rights programme and couldn't get the visa because I had to travel to have a visa interview outside Gaza, which

I couldn't do. The organisation then disqualified me. I sent them an email asking how a human rights programme could disqualify someone because they cannot enjoy their human rights. I begged to attend online, or for them to take action to support me. Nothing happened, and I lost my chance.

The stories go on and on. I can think of five friends of mine who lost master's and PhD scholarships for not being able to travel.

But dignity could be about things simpler than travelling, such as sleeping in the safety of your own home, with access to water, electricity and internet. Dignity is about having access to a toilet when you want.

Dignity, she said!

6 p.m. I remember that yesterday was my friend's birthday. I send a message: 'Hello there. I just wanted to wish you a happy birthday. I know that the situation is difficult now, but hopefully it will end soon and we can gather and celebrate together.

'If you can, get a little piece of cake and light a candle and make a wish. Wish for this nightmare to end. You never know, your wish might come true, and you will be helping many, many people.'

7 p.m. A dear person, in Norway, told me today that the snow had arrived in a blizzard and his two-year-old was amazed to see snow for the first time.

I remember the first time I saw snow. I was thirty. Imagine a thirty-year-old man from Gaza with a bunch of other Gazans seeing snow for the first time, after they got the chance to travel. We turned into young kids. Everyone around us was surprised by our childish happiness. We were throwing snowballs, making shapes and taking pictures.

I wonder how many positive first feelings I will have: a crush over someone new, visiting a new country, making a new achievement or simply watching a flower blossom. Are there any experiences left for me, or have I cashed in all of them already without even noticing?

Friday 3 November

8 a.m. I fell in love with the song 'Killing Me Softly with His Song' in my early twenties. I realised back then that my mother, too, had fallen in love with the same song at almost the same age. My mother, may she rest in peace, always shared with me her love for music, art and theatre. We also loved Abba.

The things we inherit and share with our parents are beautiful. But these days, I would have rather inherited dual nationality from my mother than love of the same songs. Today, we heard the news about some holders of dual nationalities leaving the Gaza Strip. I am very happy for them; at least they will be safe. But what about those who are left behind? Don't we deserve to be safe?

The stories of some of those who have left or are expecting to leave have started flooding in. I have heard about a man who was able to take his wife, children and parents, but could not take his siblings. They were all devastated. I have also heard about a teenage girl living with her divorced mother in Gaza who has another nationality from her father, who lives abroad. Her mother does not have the nationality. The girl has refused to leave without her mother, no matter what.

10 a.m. People in the area we're staying in are hanging big sheets between buildings on the opposite sides of small streets. This means there is more shade for people to sit under, especially boys and men, leaving more space for women to be comfortable at home.

On my way to the pharmacy this morning, I see a group of teenage boys trying to get their ball, which is stuck above the hanging cover. They throw their slippers at the cover, hoping it will move the ball. They are laughing as they try to retrieve it. I guess for a few minutes these young boys have forgotten about the misery we are going through and are enjoying the moment.

I always ask myself what the future holds for the next generation. My life, and that of those my age, has never been easy, but we have had a few better experiences than the younger generations, who have not enjoyed a healthy child-hood at all.

Noon My friend, a holder of degrees from prestigious universities, is angry when I talk to him on the phone. After finishing his PhD, he was offered a high-paying job in a European country and a possibility of getting some kind of a residency document if things went well. Instead, he decided to come back to Gaza.

'That was the stupidest decision I have ever made. Not only for me, but for my own children. Take my youngest child: he is less than six months old, and he has experienced evacuation, living in fear and lack of food. Is this the life I want for him?'

3 p.m. Another friend, who evacuated to one of the schools at first, couldn't handle the situation. Her family has been lucky – after a week, they found an apartment with three other families. She tells me that even though the situation is difficult, it is nothing compared to staying at the school with thousands of people. They are blessed enough to have access to food and water, but many other things are missing.

'The cold weather is approaching, and when we evacuated, we took only light clothes with us,' she says. 'Now, we cover the children with our clothes. We are afraid to go out and buy clothes for the children. It is not safe. No one thought the situation would be this long.'

7 p.m. One of the most annoying situations we Gazans find ourselves in is when we are calming other people, instead of the opposite happening. Ahmad has received a call from a friend abroad. His friend was crying and was very worried about us. He started calming her down and telling her: 'It is not that bad, we are alive.'

Minutes before the phone conversation, Ahmad was saying he was too tired to stand, that he would pay $1 million to sleep in a safe place for eight hours. Minutes ago, we were sharing the daily suffering of getting water. This is Ahmad, helpful Ahmad, who hears the continuous miseries of many people he knows who have lost their homes and have had to evacuate. And he tells her it is not that bad!

The emotional stress this puts on him is unbelievable. When I start reflecting on my own experiences, I realise that I do the same. While texting with a relative abroad, I lie about many details related to safety, or whether we have access to food and water. I understand Ahmad's actions, but I just feel very sorry for him – and for myself.

10 p.m. Lying on the couch, wondering how many nights I will spend away from home and my normal life, I start humming 'Killing Me Softly'. I think that I want to be killed softly with kindness, happiness and love. I don't want to be killed aggressively with weapons and bombs.

I want to die peacefully, at a very old age, after having spent a beautiful life and achieving all the dreams I wanted to make true.

And most ~~importantly, I want to live.~~

Saturday 4 November

9.30 a.m. We finally find a vet where we can take Manara to have the remaining injections. It is forty-five minutes' walk away. These days, you are more likely to find $1,000 in the street before finding a car willing to give you a ride. I go with Ahmad, with Manara in the bag. She does not resist.

On our way, we pass two schools where people have evacuated to. All I need is to take one look to see how horrible the situation is. Thousands of people are in the schools. The classrooms are full, with laundry hanging in front. The playground is packed with men and children. On the entrance of the second school, a handwritten piece of paper reads: 'The school is full, there is no space for any evacuating family. We are sorry.'

We finally reach the vet, and he tells us there is no need to give the remaining shot to Manara. He says that her eye is ruined, and all we need to do for the other one is to use eye drops. He does not approve of giving her anti-flea medicine because she has scars all over her body.

The vet has no food left or cat litter, but he directs us to another shop, which takes another ten minutes of walking to reach. When we arrive, I feel shocked; there is a lot of destruction around the place. I am scared.

We go into the shop and buy the food and litter. I see a number of birds, fish and one hamster. The owner tells us he has lost many animals because of the bombing. As for the fish, he tries to turn on the water filter for an hour every day to keep the water clean. At the door, I see a big blanket covered with bread leftovers. He says his neighbour dries these for pigeon feed.

Noon Since Manara has chosen to sleep in an old carton, I go to buy her a box. Finding a box is easy, but finding a blanket to put in it is not. There are almost no blankets or covers left. It takes me more than an hour of walking and asking at almost every shop. One seller offers me a place to wait while he fetches a blanket from his own home. I refuse and thank him.

Finally, I find a bed cover, one that comes with two pillowcases. On my way back, I remember that I don't have enough cash on me; it's a long way to the only functioning ATM machine. Recently, my bank announced that any shop with a Visa card machine can be used to withdraw money without commission. Unfortunately, only one shop offers the option of withdrawing cash – and they take commission. A big one.

2 p.m. I don't remember the last time I saw my sister eating. The grandmother hasn't made any bread for the past two days. So, when my sister asks if I can get her some *saj* bread, I go immediately.

For regular bread, people wait all day long, but *saj* bread is different. It is a very thin bread that is not enough to fill someone's stomach, so, in these times, people won't buy it because it's not the best option. Thinking of this, I imagine I won't have to wait, but I'm wrong. I wait for one hour and five minutes to buy five pieces of bread.

While waiting, I see an old colleague. She used to fight with her husband all the time. We heard more about their marital problems than about work. All the time people would be trying to fix things between them, and she would always say she will definitely leave him.

Today, I saw both of them. They were wearing dirty clothes, walking with their children, but they were hand in hand. They looked happy! Did the misery force them to disregard all their differences and focus on love?

Not everything I saw was beautiful. I saw a boy wearing a pair of shoes at least two sizes bigger than his feet. He couldn't move easily. Another guy I know, a bank employee who always wears suits, was wearing a torn T-shirt with dirty pyjama bottoms. He looked exhausted.

5.15 p.m. Yesterday, while walking with Ahmad, we saw a small black cat. Ahmad brought a piece of luncheon meat and fed it. I told him an animal lover once told me that even cats face discrimination; some people offer food and help to 'brighter-coloured' cats and ignore the black ones.

It is almost dark. I remember that I need to get something important. I go down immediately. By now, most shops are closed and almost no one is in the street.

While walking, I see the black cat I saw yesterday on the ground, with blood coming out of its mouth. It seems like a car hit its jaw, and it is unable to even move. I go quickly and pick it up. I ask a man if he can give me the nylon bag he is holding to put the cat in, and I take it home. Is it dying? I have no idea. I just can't leave it alone.

When I enter the room we are staying in, the kids are with their mum and my sister. I order them to leave the room so they don't see the injured cat. When my sister sees it, she says: 'No, no, not another one.'

'But it is injured. I can't leave it.'

My sister holds the cat, and blood starts running over her hands. She brings one of the new pillowcases and covers the cat. She also tries to give it some water. The cat is in horrible shape, breathing heavily and unable to move, while bleeding from its mouth.

For two hours, we try to contact a vet. The connection is extremely bad; you need to call for hours until you get through. The first vet says he has no medical equipment or material with him at his home, and it is very dangerous to go out at night. There is nothing he can do until tomorrow morning.

'Just give it some water. If it is external bleeding, there is a possibility it will survive. If it is internal, there is nothing we can do.'

The second doctor tells us that he is in another area, and even if we are crazy enough and willing to go, he does not know how to describe the location well, especially as the people who were hosting him have left.

There is nothing we can do. We give it water, cover it with a pillowcase and sit down, praying. I pray that if it is destined to live, it stays strong and doesn't suffer. If not, I pray that it dies quickly, without pain.

9 p.m. I walked for hours today. The soles of my feet are killing me. I look at the cat and realise that we will need to wait for at least thirteen hours before a doctor can see it. This is unbearable.

For no reason, I decide its name will be Jackie. I am not sure why I assume it is a she. If it is a he, it will be Jack.

Hearing the bombing outside, I think that this is going to be another fearful night, and it is going to be long, very long, for us – and for Jackie.

Sunday 5 November

5 a.m. Jackie, the bleeding and unconscious cat I found yesterday, made it through the night. We did not sleep. We put it in the box we got for Manara. It was breathing heavily; we kept it warm, and my sister gave it water. I never thought it would make it.

I put Jackie in the cat bag and leave at 9.15 to reach the vet's clinic at 10. When I arrive, there are several people before me with their pets. The most common complaint is: 'My cat hasn't eaten anything for almost a week, and it is getting aggressive, which has never happened before.'

The doctor explains that evacuation means they are out of their comfort zone. Also, at the evacuation places, whether it is a house or a school, there are at least thirty to forty people, and everyone wants to 'play with the cat', so it stresses them out.

The doctor checks Jackie and says the situation is critical. Till now, it hasn't opened its eyes and is in a state similar to a coma. The doctor gives it three shots and says we should give it water and a children's liquid food supplement, using a syringe, every two to three hours.

'Will it make it?' I ask.

'It all depends on its response in the coming days,' the vet says. 'By the way, you have to bring it in for at least two days for the rest of the injections.'

At least we have some hope. And it turns out that Jackie is a he, so from now on we shall call him Jack.

11.30 a.m. On my way back, I meet a guy I know, and I am shocked by his look.

'My hair, right?' he says, noticing my confused look.

'I am sorry, but . . .'

'I know – it turned grey! Within three weeks, just like that.'

I saw him a month ago, and he had a few grey hairs only. But now, most of his hair is grey! I talk to a friend later, and she says the same thing happened to her brother. Do stress, fear and sadness turn your hair grey in a month? If I had access to good internet, I would have googled it.

One thing I am sure of is that this time has successfully added wrinkles to our faces – in my case, lines under my eyes and circles of darkness. For the first time, the veins of my feet are popping out like an old man's. This experience has taken many years of our lives, past years and years to come. The question is: how many more years will we lose?

12.30 p.m. I am surprised to see a jewellery shop open. Who would buy jewellery these days? Is it safe to open this shop with the thousands of people passing by? I hear two guys talking about it, and they point something out: the owner is not showing any pieces of jewellery. He is not selling gold, he is buying gold.

People don't have money, and the only way to survive for some of them is to sell their jewellery. What better time to buy those pieces for cheap prices? I feel horrible about the whole situation, yet a part of me feels good that some people have an option to get money, even if this means losing some of their jewellery.

I receive a phone call from my friend to check on me. He shares the story of his neighbour, who decided to stay with his elderly father in their apartment in Gaza City, while his family went south. 'They barely have contact with him. His father's health is deteriorating. The horror they are facing is unbelievable. They don't have enough food or water. His family here is dying with every second away from him.'

5 p.m. My friend starts discussing with me the situation after the nightmare is over. She is worried about all the people who will go back to their areas but will be homeless; or those who will have to spend thousands of dollars to fix their houses to meet the bare minimum standards of living. She speaks about the emotional distress every Gazan will have to deal with.

But she is thinking about the aftermath, which means that she thinks it will be over, and even over soon. It's not that I lack this optimism, but from what I see, hear and learn, it is going to take a much longer time.

9 p.m. We lose the connection again. Whatever. What else do we have to lose? We have lost our dignities, our lives, our memories . . . the connection is no big deal any more.

I recall a poem I read once by Sabrina Benaim, in her book *Depression & Other Magic Tricks*. She wrote:

I held hands with my sadness,
Sang it songs in the shower,
Fed it lunch,

Got it drunk
And put it to bed early.

Is that what my friend and other people are thinking? Putting their sadness to bed early so they can steal some time to spend with hope? If I put sadness to bed early, what about fear? What about grief? What about sorrow? What about exhaustion?

For me, I am still in phase one, or maybe in phase zero, with my sadness. I am still trying to be face to face with it and tell 'him' that I see him. Just like that. It is going to be a very long journey just to realise the amount of sadness I have within.

If we get out of this, I want to be sad for a long time, to hold my sadness in my hands, hug it tight, and then maybe try to move on with my life, or what is left of it.

Tuesday 7 November

My friend has no name.

I met him during a difficult period of my life. I had started a new job and was not sure I was ready to return to work. But his presence was all I needed. After the first week, I sent him a message, thanking him for being a very kind and helpful person.

My friend was a great father of two girls. In the conservative society we live in, he faced pressure for not having a boy. At social occasions, some people would wish him a boy to 'hold your name'. However, he was extremely happy and proud of his daughters. He told me several times that they were more than enough, they were the biggest gift he had ever received. He wanted them to be strong and independent. At work, they would call him to discuss anything. I would hear him telling them how much he loved them.

People in the office called us 'the duo' or 'the buddies'. We would spend our breaks together, talking and laughing, discussing issues important and silly. He had a unique laugh. One time, I told him that I was planning to buy a mug for myself. The next day, a nice mug appeared in my office, a gift from him. And every time we went on a break, he would laugh about me using the 'mug he bought with his own money'. Even after I left for another job, I took his mug with me, and I would send him messages from time to time, wishing we could share a break together.

My friend loved helping others. Every month, he would buy chicken, vegetables and other food items from his salary and give them to poor families. At work, he never hesitated to help colleagues; he did not care about rivalries or showing off his skills. Everyone spoke fondly of him.

Once a month, we would go walking together for an hour or two. Not for the exercise, but for the opportunity to have one of the wonderful discussions we used to share.

Two weeks ago, he sent me a message to say he was looking for a place to move to. 'We cannot handle the displacement in schools or at hospitals. I need any decent place to take my family. Otherwise, I won't be able to leave Gaza City.' There were no places left. The last message from him was a couple of days ago: he told me how tired he was and how surviving every day is a miracle.

* * *

My sister hears the news from someone in her social circle. I immediately call a mutual friend, who calms me down and tells me that it was not him. 'It cannot be him, I have spoken to him recently,' she says. I try to call his mobile, but cannot reach him.

Fifteen minutes later, I receive a call from her, crying: 'It might be him.'

An hour later, it is confirmed. My friend, his wife and his two daughters are no longer alive.

I do not cry; not one tear falls. I call our mutual friend again and I tell her that great people like him will live in our memories. We will always talk about what a wonderful person and father he was.

After we end the call, I go to the balcony and I try to call him again. Maybe it was a rumour; hopefully it was a bad joke. *Please, be alive. Please, be alive.*

I don't know how I feel.

Yesterday, we were able to wash our clothes by hand. I go upstairs to the roof, take the laundry down. It is not even dry, but I do not care. I fold the laundry.

I stand up, look at the room: there are lots of things that need to be changed and moved. My sister says nothing. I rearrange the whole room.

I need to breathe. I need to be alone. During these horrible times, you cannot be alone. You have no space to process feelings; you cannot even grieve a dead person.

I go to the toilet, close the door and sit on the floor. I can't cry, and I can't breathe either. I calm myself and go out.

I find the children in our room. They speak about every-thing. The youngest plays at being mother and prepares peas and cakes for her 'children'; the middle one speaks about wanting to travel like his cousin did and 'see the world'; the oldest speaks about the gifts she received from her aunt when she was abroad.

I listen and can't stop thinking about my friend's daugh-ters. I was sure, and I always told him, that people who were raised well like his daughters are the positive seeds of the future. Children like them are the ones who make this world a better place. Unfortunately, they never had the chance.

Hearing about people that you don't know dying is one thing, but losing someone close to you, someone you shared secrets with, someone whose energy would shine . . . this is one of the most awful things you can go through.

How many people are we going to lose before we get out of this nightmare? How many dreams will die? How many more great people stolen from their loved ones?

My friend died in Gaza City. I cannot be there for his funeral. Will he have a decent burial? Or will his and his family's bodies be left until the whole situation is over. I will not be able to hug his loved ones and tell them how sorry I am.

My friend has no name because my friend is everyone's friend. He is the kind colleague at work, the great father you see in the park and the helpful person in any community.

I wonder how scared my friend was. Was he hugging his girls when they all died?

Wednesday 8 November

2 a.m. My sister has a fever. She cannot raise her head and is hallucinating. We put wet towels on her head, hoping her temperature will go down. We cannot call anyone or go anywhere for help.

I am grateful the situation is not dangerous. Last night, Ahmad told us about his relative, who had to go to the hospital for problems with her blood pressure. He went with her and was shocked by how terrible the situation was. Families that fled to the hospital were everywhere, not only outside, but inside and in the hallways. Putting their mattresses down and sleeping, while doctors and nurses moved through them. After waiting for hours, the doctor said that Ahmad's relative needs to be monitored for a couple of hours to make sure she is stable. There was no place for her to sit, so she waited outside the hospital.

Each of our cats is lying on one of the couches, except Jack, who is in his box in the place where we are staying. He started trying to get out of it, which is great, but required complete attention from my side. We are sure he cannot see. During the days, I pass by kittens in the streets and cats that seem sick, but I cannot take them with me; we already have four cats, and two are in a bad condition. I remind myself we cannot save every single one, and hopefully, they will eventually survive.

I wonder about the doctors in the hospitals, receiving numbers of cases that they cannot handle even under normal circumstances. I am sure they have had to choose which person to save, which to provide care to. I cannot imagine the horrible situation they are going through right now, and the horror they will live with when all of this is over.

5.30 a.m. My sister has started getting better. I did not have a minute of sleep in over twenty-four hours. She woke up and tried to move a little, and I decided to close my eyes. Fifteen minutes later, I hear her screaming: 'The cat is not here.' I open my eyes immediately. I check: Manara and Jack are in the room, the young cat is, too. Oh my God, it is the older one that's missing.

'Are you sure?' I ask.

'Yes, I checked several times. She was on the balcony when we heard a very loud sound; the other cats got afraid and came in. She may have jumped.'

It is almost completely dark outside. I put the other cats in the carriers, and we both go down, looking for her. My sister is running like crazy, crying her eyes out. I am sure we have lost her cat. We search everywhere, using the flashlight on my mobile. I pray that we find her; she has been through a lot of fear already, and now this, being alone. She must be terrified.

A neighbour leans out of a window and tells my sister that she saw 'a white body' moving towards one of the empty lots around us. The neighbour's children, aged seven and nine, come out to start looking with us.

We are all running everywhere, not sure where we are heading. Finally, the older kid shouts: 'I found her, I found her!' My sick sister who has a fever, runs so fast. I am closer than her, yet I arrive later.

We find our cat, hiding under a bush, not moving an inch. She is terrified. My sister hugs her, crying, apologising for not taking care of her.

We go back to the room. My eyes are wide open. Even though I am grateful that our cat is back, I know for sure, after my adrenaline, that I will not enjoy a minute of sleep for at least another twenty-four hours.

Noon My friend calls me to check on us. She seems annoyed. 'We have gone back to primitive times. We have no gas any more, so my whole family went outside and we started burning wood to cook with. Can you imagine? We had our lunch by burning wood. And this is not a fun camping experience, this is the situation from now on. I am not sure what else we can endure. The situation is getting much worse.'

3 p.m. We are overwhelmed by the number of people who are dying. Some we know, some are close to our friends, and some are close to us. The feeling of helplessness is overwhelming me, and I am unable to cry. I am unable to act based on my sadness; I am just acting 'normal', which is worrying me a lot.

I decide to listen to a love song. If this period is not the best for love songs, which is? The song is on the soundtrack of a movie: 'When Adam hugged Hanan . . . he had the whole world in his hands . . . He became human.'

I couldn't help but think about a young couple I met days ago in the street. They got married six weeks ago. They had no 'big story'; simply, a guy met a girl, they fell in love, everything went well, their families supported their relationship, and *voilà*, they got married. They did not know that the first chapter of their story, the honeymoon, would involve fleeing to save their lives and testing their love during these tough times. Instead of spending lovely time together and buying roses, they were trying to buy clothes because they couldn't wash the ones they have left.

Another couple I know, who have been married for a few months, met abroad, while both were on a scholarship to complete their master's. Everyone talked about their love story. The husband was killed few days ago, leaving his wife and a promising future behind. I cannot imagine how a twenty-something woman would process the experience of being a widow.

5 p.m. I receive a call from an international number. It is my friend's sister, asking me to check on her brother and family since no one is answering her calls or messages. Though there is a connection, it is extremely bad. We send SMS messages, yet sometimes they never reach; to call someone, you try for almost an hour before getting through to them, if you are lucky; and the internet connection (the mobile data) is almost unavailable – I receive messages five to six hours after they were sent, and sometimes the next day. The funny thing is that it is easier to make an international call than a local one. After three hours, I am able to check on her family. They are safe.

7 p.m. Manara is sitting on the top of the couch I am sitting on. Comparing Manara to Jack has made her seem healthier, even though she still needs a lot of care.

I apologised to her for having to give her box to Jack, since he is very sick. I started describing what her life would be like if she were at our home right now. I told her that she would have had many spaces she would have enjoyed. And I told her about the cat toys and beds we once had.

I noticed the tone I was using to talk about the house. As if I haven't been there in many years, as if I am talking about a dream rather than a real place I was at almost a month ago.

I really miss my home. I miss my life. I miss myself.

Thursday 9 November

8 a.m. Falafel is one of the most popular traditional foods in Gaza. We call it 'the poor people's food' because it is cheap. Palestinians who travel abroad are surprised at the prices of falafel sandwiches, and I know I speak for everyone in Gaza when I say that we believe the ones made in Gaza are the best.

Luckily for us, in the area we evacuated to there were two shops selling falafel. Unfortunately, one closed soon after we arrived because the owner ran out of gas. But we are among the few neighbourhoods that still have the luxury of getting falafel. The remaining shop works two shifts, one in the morning and one from 3 to 5 p.m. They no longer sell sandwiches, only falafel, since getting bread is very difficult. I usually go in the evening, because until recently we didn't eat breakfast. I would wait for about forty-five minutes to get my order, but it is OK: now you have to wait for everything, if it is available.

Today, I decide to get some falafel for breakfast. I thought I went early, but the line is so long. I am told that people start queueing shortly after 6 a.m. to secure a spot. I try to count how many people are ahead of me and get tired after eighty-five. I see my friend, so we stand together and decide to spend 'the journey of getting falafel' together. I send a message to my sister, telling her it will probably take me a long time to return.

8.30 a.m. 'In the sea?' I ask, surprised.

'Yes,' my friend answers.

We are talking about how miserable the situation is for people displaced in schools and hospitals. While waiting in line, I noticed a lot of flies buzzing around the neck of a man standing ahead of us. It is no surprise – people haven't had access to hygiene facilities for more than a month now. Only the lucky ones have access to water, or at least money to buy deodorant.

My friend tells me that some displaced people who are next to the sea go there to wash themselves. 'You see mostly men and children. But even women go there to clean themselves. I know how annoying it is to have the remains of the salty seawater over your body, but it is better than being filthy.'

9 a.m. We have moved a little forward. My friend starts having a conversation with two men about six or seven places ahead of us. I take the opportunity to make some phone calls, checking on my friends. I can't reach most of them due to the unreliable connection – at least that is what I tell myself, trying not to think about any bad thing that could have happened to them overnight. Finally, I get through to one who is a pharmacist.

Pharmacists these days are suffering. In the absence of effective hospitals and clinics, and with the difficulties in seeing a doctor, people go to pharmacies for medical support.

Every time I go to the pharmacy, which is a lot these days, I see pharmacists checking children, adults' aches and pains, and hearing different symptoms of sick people, some of which are very complicated. People hope to get something to help them survive until they can see a doctor.

142

My friend tells me about a customer of his who called to remind him that she owed him some money, and she wanted him to forgive her in case something bad happened to her. 'I was surprised. I told her that of course I forgave her, and we would meet after this is all over and she can pay me. Unfortunately, two days later, she and her family died.'

10 a.m. Standing in line, several arguments start about people jumping the queue. The owner of the shop has to come out and maintain order. It feels as if he is a school principal, but I understand that he wants things to move smoothly. Apparently, this situation has been going on for a month now. I was lucky not to eat breakfast before.

The shop owner is a kind guy. He makes his shop available to everyone to come and charge their phones and UPS batteries. One time, I was passing and saw hundreds of devices connected to cords inside and outside the shop.

I think of the owner of another shop I was at the other day. I joked with him: 'I bet us people who came from Gaza City or the north are annoying you now, so many of us and all our needs.' He smiled and said: 'Not at all. If we don't welcome you in the difficult times, when will we? You are people in need, and it is our duty to help.' I later found out that he and his wife had left their home and moved in with their son to allow families from Gaza City to stay in his place.

10.30 a.m. We are still waiting in line. I ask my friend about his family, and he says they are OK. He says: 'I was talking to a friend, and he wanted to tell me about something that happened to my house. I shut him up and asked him not to finish his sentence. If something happened to my house, I don't want to know about it now. If we get out of this alive, I will deal with it later. I have no space to mourn the loss of my house.'

11 a.m. After standing in line for hours, they let groups of people enter, buy their falafel and leave. Now, we are inside with about twenty other people. No line any more, so everyone tries to get their order in first. Everyone is frustrated. I hear a man saying that if it were up to him, he wouldn't even eat, but he needs to get breakfast for his children, 'and there are no other options'.

11.30 a.m. We get the falafel. On our way out, the people still waiting jokingly start shouting 'Congratulations!' and saying phrases usually said when someone has a new baby.

Since the beginning of the whole situation, I have not taken a single picture of myself or anyone else. I believe that pictures are a way to keep great memories to look back on, but from these days there is nothing great or beautiful to remember.

However, I ask my friend if we could take a picture. 'Looking like this?' he asks. I say yes. I suggest we get the falafel in the picture, but he refuses – he has boundaries. We put the falafel down and take the picture. I smile from ear to ear. I am not happy, and I am not pretending to be. But I have a positive feeling. I don't know what it is, it is just that

I saw my friend, we talked, we are still alive. It is a new day (or, to be more precise, the middle of a new day now), and – we got falafel!

Sunday 12 November

Midnight I am wide awake. Not because of fear, exhaustion or the lack of a moment of peace we have been experiencing for more than a month now, but because I can't stop thinking about the phone call I had last night. My friend lost her brother. She was devastated. I tried to talk to her but couldn't. I was able to reach friends around her. 'She is grateful that they found the body of her brother in one piece, unlike the others, whose bodies were cut into several parts,' one told me.

Is this what we've come to? Praying that we die in one piece? Has dying in brutal circumstances become the inevitable destiny of Gazans?

I remember a story told in my mother's family. A story about two women who had a feud for more than forty years about which of their sons was buried in a certain grave. Both bodies were cut into pieces, and to this day the truth is not known. Each of the ladies would go to the graveyard and mourn her lost child. 'But why does it matter?' I remember asking.

'It is all that matters,' an old neighbour answered. He said knowing their loved ones were buried in a dignified manner, in a known spot, made them feel sure that they were in a 'safe place, taken care of', and it helped them to let go and start the journey of moving on.

One of the two ladies died past the age of eighty-five; the other one is still alive to this day. I am sure that the one who died is no longer angry with the other mother, because now she is with her son in a much better place – away from graveyards, away from death, away from sadness, away from the cruelty of this world. She is hugging him, and he is very happy, because he is finally safe with his mother.

I wonder how many decades it will take a lot of Gazans to process the agony of not knowing where their loved ones are buried, or the fact that they couldn't have a final look at them, hold their hands and say goodbye.

8.30 a.m. He was not my friend, but some people just grow to become a part of your life. He was the head waiter of my favourite cafe. I had known him since I was a university student, when the restaurant was very small and not well known. With time, he became the symbol of the place. When he was not around, people would ask for him. Some would go only when he was working. The restaurant expanded and he would move from one branch to the other, and people would choose to dine where he was working.

He had beautiful green eyes. Everyone loved him. He listened to his customers; in a way, he was a kind of therapist. He would give advice, guidance and support. If he recommended a certain dish, we would order it immediately. If he advised you not to order your favourite meal, we would trust him.

Two years ago, his eldest son graduated from high school. The waiter was very happy; he told us that his son will study journalism. He mentioned that in addition to him loving what he does, he works very hard, many shifts, just to secure a good life for his family.

I am walking in the street when my friend calls me and tells me he has been killed. I stop walking. Not him . . . no, no, no. I stay silent in the middle of the street.

Though he was not a friend of mine, he was a part of my life, a part of the many happy memories I have. I wish I could have protected him. I wish I could have kept him and his loved ones safe.

I want to cry, yet I keep silent and continue walking.

9 a.m. Today is cloudy, which is good for those on the street since they won't be burned by the sun. However, this means that no one will be able to charge their devices. The only source of energy these days is solar, and just a few families or shops have solar power, so all the neighbours and evacuated families go there to charge their devices, to have connection with the world, to remind themselves they are still alive.

Today, we couldn't charge our devices. Another day to forget we are still alive.

10 a.m. I am running out of one of the medicines I take. I had good amounts with me, but after a month, most of it is gone. I go to the pharmacy to buy more. The pharmacist has only six tablets left. I thank him and leave without taking them. He advises me to take them, but I refuse. I want two or three packs, not a couple of pills.

I start my journey looking for my medicine. I walk for almost four hours. I enter every single pharmacy on the way. Sixteen pharmacies, none has my medicine. I admit that it is my mistake, I should have bought extra since the whole situation started, but I did not think it would continue this long. Nobody did.

2 p.m. I go back to the first pharmacy, hoping they still have the six pills. They do. I take them and leave.

As I am passing a long line of people waiting to buy *saj* bread, the people in the queue are encouraging the young guy selling the bread to be faster. One tells him: 'I wish you get married soon.' Another says jokingly: 'I hope you fall in love with a beautiful displaced woman and marry her.'

The guy smiles shyly and continues his work. I remember my grandmother telling us that her grandmother had to get married at the age of fourteen to a bread-maker, just to be able to feed her family.

We are not there yet, or at least I am privileged not to see the misery others are living in. But I don't think we are far away from people doing things against their desires just to secure some bread.

7 p.m. Ahmad joins us in the room. He tells us that today he saw his friend who is an artist. He was in the street, boiling some water to make tea to sell. His friend had no gas canister; instead, he was burning wood. Ahmad was surprised to see the man using the frames of his own portraits to burn. 'I need to make some money, I have a family to feed,' the friend told him.

Even wood is becoming scarce, and some are selling it to be used to boil water and in cooking. What else is left to be sold? Air?

9 p.m. My sister has rarely left the room since we evacuated. In normal times, she is a social butterfly and very active in the community. Since the whole situation started, she has only gone out when it is very important. Today, she decided to take the young girls for a walk. She took the eldest grand-daughter and her female cousin. 'We are suffocated,' they had told her the previous day.

At night, she tells me how happy the girls were. She says they had the biggest smiles over their faces, glad to be out after such a long time. They did not do anything special, she says, just walked and bought some hair scrunchies.

But my sister is sad that a good deal of their talk was about this friend who lost her house, the other who lost family members, and the ones who evacuated and with whom they have lost contact. 'Is this the childhood they deserve?' she asks.

Not only little girls, but women in general face double the suffering. During these times, men usually get the chance to go out to get necessary stuff, while women find themselves stuck in the house with many other families or at schools with little to no space. At the schools, I would see men standing or sitting outside to get some air, but would rarely see a woman.

10 p.m. Lying on the couch, I can't stop thinking about a quote someone shared with me. It says: 'We need enormous pockets, pockets big enough for our families, and our friends, and even the people who aren't on our lists, people we've never met but still want to protect. We need pockets for boroughs and for cities, and a pocket that could hold the universe.'

I wish I had big pockets, to keep my loved ones, my friends and the animals safe. I wish I could keep the waiters, the artists, the students, the street sellers and the teachers safe. I wish I could keep the streets and the kindergartens and the restaurants and every single place that witnessed a happy memory safe. And most of all, I wish I could be held tight in someone else's big pocket . . . to feel safe.

Tuesday 14 November

7.45 a.m. It is raining. The weather has become very cold suddenly. When we evacuated, we were wearing summer clothes – I evacuated in shorts and T-shirt. I bought a jacket yesterday because I anticipated this would happen. I wear the jacket and cover myself with a blanket.

My heart goes out to all those in schools, hospitals, and the ones who have recently fled and haven't found a roof to sit under yet. What are parents thinking of right now – are they hugging their children tight so they won't feel the cold? How many people will be sick? How many will survive?

It started getting colder a while ago, but not as strong as today. Two days ago, my sister was talking to her friend and her mother who evacuated to one of the schools. The mother, who fled wearing light prayer clothes, told her she had just a light blanket that she covers her stomach with to sleep at night.

How long will this misery last?

9 a.m. Finally, a shy sun appears. I go out on to the street, after being one of the few who had stayed inside. People try to find things that will help them survive. I look closely at people's clothes. Most men are still in shorts, and all of them are wearing short-sleeved T-shirts. Women are wearing light clothes as well. Seeing torn clothes on people no longer surprises me. The streets are muddy, but almost everyone is wearing slippers.

10 a.m. While buying some stuff, I meet a friend waiting in line to buy *saj* bread. 'I have been standing here for over two hours,' he says. 'In the rain?' I ask, surprised. He just gives me a weak smile.

Two young boys appear, aged around nine and ten. They are holding a large amount of bread they brought from elsewhere – maybe their own home, or someone made it for them – and they want to sell it. Once the people in the line see them, they leave the queue and run towards them.

The boys are covered by the wave of men. Each man wants the boys to take his money and give him bread. One boy is covering his head with his hand. A man holds the other boy by the collar and screams at him to give him the bread. My friend is there, too, trying to reach one of the boys but failing.

I stand still, shocked at the scene. Suddenly, everyone comes running back to the line. Then I see one guy taking all the bread. 'What happened?' I ask my friend.

'You see that guy over there? He threw a big bill at the boys and bought the whole lot. I have lost ten places in the line. I will have to wait another half-hour.'

At the beginning, almost nobody bought the *saj* bread because it was too thin. Now, people are buying anything, if they have the money. The situation is getting worse by the second.

*   *   *

I go to a shop . . . and find biscuits! I can't believe it. I notice that people take the biscuits, go to the cashier to pay, then return them – the biscuits are on sale at eight times the original price. Because I am blessed and have money, I can buy some. My savings are evaporating, but all I care about is surviving these days.

One topic that always comes up in any discussion with friends is the terrible feeling of guilt – of having money while others don't; of having a roof over your head and some food while others don't; of being alive while others are dying.

I hear a woman in the street saying that we will not die of fear but of sadness. I don't remember a time when my heart was not aching. Even in the positive moments, there is a feeling inside that we will not make it out alive.

Noon Thousands of families are still fleeing towards our area. Every day I hear one horrible story after another. I hear about a man whose mother couldn't walk far; they did their best to find a wheelchair for her, but couldn't. So they brought an office chair with wheels, and he slowly pushed his mother for hours.

I see an old neighbour who is looking for food. 'My parents lost their house, I lost my apartment, I lost my company. If we make it out alive, what will we go back to?'

I can't believe my ears. This young guy was a risk-taker. When he couldn't find a job, he decided not to give up and started his own company, using his technical and programming skills. He spent over two years trying to establish his company; finally, he started, and was contacting everyone he knew to promote his work.

'Our main concern is water,' he says. 'My father [who holds a PhD] is the toilet police. We are not allowed to flush the toilet every time. He ordered us to put big bottles in the cistern so it does not fill with water, and only a little comes down when we flush.'

7 p.m. Will it make any difference if I write about the air-strikes and bombing? Is it worth it to write about the two very close to us, in streets that I, and hundreds of people, pass six times a day to buy our stuff? Shall I write about the constant feeling of fear for our lives and the ones we are responsible for? Should I talk about the helplessness and despair we are all going through? Does it matter?

8 p.m. It is raining. It is cold. The thunder is very strong. I have a friend who has always been a fan of winter. She hated summers. I receive a message from her: 'This is the first time in forty years I hate the winter.'

When I was in my twenties, I would always wait for the rain, to walk in it. Each of my friends had accompanied me in one of those crazy moments. We would not even hold umbrellas. A friend reminds me of when we went out to eat *knafeh* in the rain. 'How crazy were we? But those times were worth it.'

9 p.m. I turn on some music, without wearing headphones. I don't care if it is late. I hear a song I love. It is weird how you listen to a song hundreds of times but never focus on the lyrics. For the first time, I listen to what the singer is saying:

155

*It turned out there is a day! So why am I suffering . . . far in
the darkness?*

*If only the light gets through the big walls . . . I belong to a
special place*

Will our rainy nights end? Will we see the light again?

Thursday 16 November

8 a.m. My dream is simple. I want to sit in one of my favourite restaurants in Gaza City, admiring the beautiful blue sea. I would order chicken pasta with lots of appetisers and a salad (you know, to stay healthy). I will be in the company of my friends; we will talk about our mundane lives, complain about our work and discuss our favourite TV shows. I will order hot chocolate and get a surprise, like every time, when I discover how many calories it contains. When my friends leave, I will pick up my book and continue reading. All I want is a quiet day in Gaza City.

My sister is talking to a friend of hers, describing how bad the situation has become in the schools and other places that people fled to. 'The man was cooking at the entrance of the school while the sewage water was running next to him,' she says. 'The scene, and the smell, made me want to vomit.'

These days, I always ask my friends about what they had for lunch. The options are very limited:

'We had biscuits and water.'

'We had eggplants and cucumbers.'

It does not matter to me what they ate, as long as they had something to eat. Unfortunately, not everyone is lucky enough. Some are sleeping without anything entering their stomach for the whole day. The prices are rocketing.

When we first evacuated to the third family's house, they used to cook something different every day. Now, things are less available. The only falafel shop has closed its doors due to not having any gas canisters left. We have been regularly eating cheese and thyme sandwiches. They are delicious. The grandmother of the third family bakes every couple of days. And from time to time, I stand in line and get some *saj* bread. I couldn't be more grateful.

9 a.m. Every morning, thousands of people are in the streets, looking for what they need: food, medicine, blankets, heavy clothes. I saw a mother screaming at her young son in the middle of the street. It turned out that he had got distracted, and she had been looking for him for almost an hour.

'How would I find you if you got lost?' she screamed. Other women were calming her down.

These days, we hear many stories about parents who have lost their children, either while fleeing or in public places. Most of the evacuating people are in these new areas for the first time; they may have passed by them before, or visited, but knowing the area is really difficult when most people have lost their ability to focus due to fear, stress or lack of sleep.

I remember talking to my friend who had a new baby girl months ago. 'I know this will sound scary, but please, write on your daughter's body all the identification information in marker, just in case,' I said. He was silent for a second, then he told me that he agreed with me.

I have witnessed several times the same situation: a group of boys go out to play with a ball, and the parents, usually fathers, would go out angry and tell them to get back inside.

'If a bombing happens now, what will happen to you?! Go inside, immediately.'

Not only parents are scared, but everyone is scared for their own safety. You go to buy medicine, and you are not sure whether you will get back or not. You leave the place you are at and wonder whether it will get bombed or not.

10 a.m. The cats are doing well. Every day, I take Jack to the vet to give him the required injections.

Unfortunately, it is certain Jack cannot see. But we are grateful that he is able to walk. And now, he has started eating puréed food. Also, he started recognising the litter box; sometimes he does it in there and sometimes not. We found some disposable pads to put in the box so it will be easier to clean. Jack wants to move a lot. He uses his head and legs to make sure nothing is in his way, he even tries to climb over the couches. Sometimes he falls, other times it goes well.

Since she got lost, our big cat has been distressed. She wakes up several times while sleeping and starts meowing loudly. We tell her that we are here. Once she hears one of our voices, she goes back to sleep.

Manara has been 'sleep-compensating' for the past two days. Only when food is served does she wake, stand in line, politely, after the other cats, and wait her turn. She always gives us a grateful look. She eats and goes back to sleep. Her wounds are healing, and no lumps are coming out of her damaged eye any more.

The small cat is the craziest. When I sleep for a couple of minutes, I wake to her tail covering my nose or her big eyes looking directly into mine. She has developed what I call the 'sleeping trust position': she sleeps in a way that, if you make any move, she would fall, so you have to stay still for a long time to keep her safe. If you move, even an inch, she would be annoyed.

I believe that their presence is distracting us from a lot of the negative feelings we might have if they weren't there.

4 p.m. Everyone is fighting. People are fighting over water, bread and over nothing. The level of anxiety is reaching its peak.

My sister's friend calls her, crying. He is with his wife and two children at his brother's house. He tells her that his brother's wife is controlling everything: what they eat, how much they eat and when they can use the toilet. 'It is humiliating. She would control the breath we take if she could. But we have no other option. We have to tolerate her.'

6 p.m. There is nothing hopeful. Nobody knows anything. There are many friends who we are not sure if they are safe or not, or alive or dead. The communication is bad; many places have no internet connection, and uncertainty is high.

'How are you?' is becoming the most difficult question. We don't know how we are any more. We are not sure how we feel. And to add salt to the wound, our loved ones who are abroad ask questions like: 'What is the solution to this whole situation?'

We are like: 'Really?! The whole world is unable to solve this situation, and you think we know the answer?!'

10 p.m. When you get into the shower and you feel cold, appreciate that first drop of hot water over your body.

When you are about to eat a meal, look at the plates, give yourself time to let the beautiful smells of the food in, admire what you have, the variety of colours. And the taste.

When you are in your house, hug the walls. Yes, hug the walls. Be grateful to have a roof over your head.

Because even though these details are minor, for many, they are a dream. Believe me, if you have a good meal, access to basic needs and a normal, mundane routine, you own the whole world.

Friday 17 November

4 a.m. I have been having nightmares. I believe it is due to a variety of reasons: fear, stress, the cold weather and lack of proper sleep. I would manage to sleep for a few minutes or an hour from time to time. At first, my nightmares were about me or a loved one dying by a bomb. But now they are different: they are about not being able to find food. I have been so lucky that, till now, we have food, regardless of what it is; today, one thing is available, and tomorrow, another. This is a blessing.

This night, I dreamed about going to many shops, fancy ones. None of them had anything edible. The last one did, but the seller refused to sell to me. I kept screaming at him: 'I have money, I have money.' I woke up with half of my body off the couch I was sleeping on.

Jack the cat's health has deteriorated suddenly. We don't know why. He feels cold, even though we are covering him properly. My sister held him all night; he had his arm around hers. He refused to even drink water. I hope he gets better.

8 a.m. I go out to see if there is anything available. From time to time, I find something good. The other day, I found nuts, which was great. One time, Ahmad had his friends over; he offered them raisins, because that is what was available that time. While walking, I find a few people gathered around a man making *saj* bread. I go there directly to have a spot at the top of the line. One of the men tells me I need to write my name. I laugh. I am like: 'Yes, now we need to register to buy some *saj* bread.' He was not kidding! The seller had a notebook with him and wrote the names to maintain order. Even though I thought it was a great idea, I was in shock.

Is that the stage we have reached?

My number is forty-three, that's why there are not a lot of people gathered. Those who registered are sitting in the shade. I look around and see them sitting on the pavement. I also see a guy I worked with many years ago crouching there. I smile and go sit next to him.

Without any greetings, he looks at me and says: 'Four children. I have four children. What was I thinking?! It is true that the last two were not planned, but who brings four children into a place like Gaza? I go all day long to bring *saj*, to find milk, to get a certain medicine, to fight over water. Nobody should have children in Gaza.'

I sit on the ground, and everyone around starts sharing their experience. All the people waiting are from Gaza City. One of them is an owner of a shop in the area considered the downtown. 'I spent my whole life building my business and an excellent reputation. Now, I am not sure whether I will go back to a broken shop or a destroyed one,' he says.

The man I know stands up to check what number the *saj* seller has reached. He leaves his wallet on the ground. When he comes back, I tell him that he should be careful not to leave his stuff. 'As if it has a lot of money or anything valuable. Our lives have no value these days,' he says.

Once my turn comes and I take the *saj* bread, I turn to leave. The shop owner yells at me to 'dust my pants', since they got dirty after sitting on the pavement. I am a little way away, and maybe a little upset, so I answer loudly: 'Look at us! Look at our clothes! Does it matter if our clothes are clean or dirty? I haven't had a shower in a very long time; some sand over my pants will be an issue?!!' I continue walking, without dusting my pants, because I do not care.

The situation is getting worse by the minute. When it first escalated, my sister went to visit a woman she knew who had fled to one of the schools. My sister offered her money, but the woman refused, she said she and her family could manage. A few days ago, my sister visited her again, and when she offered her money, the woman took it. It is completely understandable: the situation is very bad, people are panicking. They want to survive. We want to survive.

11 a.m. On my way back, I meet a university professor I know. I admit that I was impressed that he had maintained a neat look despite the horrible times. I have noticed that people these days have no energy to even do the polite part of the talking, like: 'Hi, how are you?' They just start talking, as if you had been together for an hour. He looks at me and points his finger towards what I assume is Egypt. 'The minute this is over, I am leaving immediately. We call ourselves educators? What is left, and who is left to educate? We have gone back a hundred years. Our main concern will be finding a roof over our heads, not education.'

I continue moving. I see another man I know. He and his wife and children left, while his parents, siblings and others decided to stay in Gaza City. 'I feel extremely guilty for leaving them behind. I am here, "safer", while they are witnessing all kinds of suffering. I don't think I will forgive myself, because I am the oldest brother and it was my responsibility to make sure all are safe.'

3 p.m. Two positive things happened today. The first was Ahmad telling us about how the residents of one area welcomed the people who had fled with water and biscuits. Young men stood in the middle of the streets with smiles all over their faces, sending a message to those who left and are scared that they are welcome. The other thing was seeing the children feeding our cats.

However, Ahmad shared another story that was sad. He told us about some trees in one of the areas that are very old. One time, a man was imprisoned for cutting one of them down. He said that these days, the people cut those trees to find wood for cooking and to keep warm. Even though he understands why, a part of him feels sad, because those trees were a symbol of the area.

I am not sure how many other symbols of Gaza are left. If we get back, will we be able to recognise the city?

11.25 p.m. Jack did not make it.

My sister insisted that she bury him in the land next to us. Nobody goes out at night, it is dangerous, but she said: 'He deserves to be buried in a decent way. I will not wait until tomorrow morning. Can you guarantee we will be alive by then?' She goes by herself. I stay in the room.

165

We did our best to save Jack. We gave him food and medicine, we kept him warm, we took care of him, my sister held him for nights, we took him to the vet every day.

I swear, we did our best, but he did not make it.

This world is unfair.

Monday 20 November

1 p.m. Everything is expensive, except for the lives of Gazans. Two months ago, a pack of salt would have cost 25 cents; now it costs $5. In the small room with my sister, I hear Ahmad giving his father the daily prices update and what is available in the market and what is not. Ahmad's father says: 'It is better to go to the sea and extract some salt from there than buy salt from the market.'

Another 'treasure' these days is blankets. With the vicious cold and onslaught of winter, people are desperate for anything to cover themselves and their children with at night, especially those without shelter or those staying at the schools. The past four days, the prices have doubled every day. A woman I know is staying at a house where the windows were broken by the bombing. They covered the halls with nylon and cardboard. 'We have heavy blankets, but the cold is deadly,' she told me. 'We did not have a minute of sleep.'

I meet friends, and the mother tells me she is looking for instant yeast; it is used to make dough. They are staying in a house with about fifty people, and she is responsible for baking for all of them. She is old and sick, and when I ask why she is doing all the heavy work, she says that since people are hosting them, she has to do what it takes to show appreciation.

Today, I find the instant yeast, small packets that used to sell for $1 each; now they cost $9. I call to see if they want me to buy one.

2 p.m. The host family serves lunch, lentil soup. I take a sip and realise it needs salt. I feel shy to ask for some, knowing the current prices. Instead, my sister suggests that she slices in one of the lemons we have. It tastes better.

After eating, I receive a call from a friend of ours who lives abroad. She is crying so much, I can't even tell who it is until after a couple of minutes. Many people have called her and sent her messages telling her that her sister has been killed. She was trying to reach her family but couldn't. After many calls, it turned out that the person who died was someone else with the same name.

She tells me how she has had to explain to many people abroad the importance of having strong communication. They wonder, are Gazans so vain that they care more about having a good internet connection than the safety of their families? She told them that communication means people can check on their loved ones, they can hear the news, they can know where to get food and other items. Communication is not about Facebook love posts or Instagram happy pictures, it is about survival.

I receive a message. A friend of a friend says she is praying that this whole nightmare will end soon. She says how bad she feels for all the Gazan children, women and men who are going through these horrible days, and how she keeps thinking of us all the time. Even though I don't know her, her message makes me feel like someone has touched my heart with their hands. For a few seconds, I feel loved and cared for, and that is enough for the day.

5 p.m. A friend who shares my love of language sends me a link to the *New York Times'* Word of the Day. The word is 'obfuscation', and through the SMS message, he quizzes me about the meaning. He says that for the first time, he is sure I won't google it, since I have no proper internet access.

I don't know the meaning of the word – it turns out to mean 'to make things unclear'. Coincidentally, the verb 'obfuscate' applies to the future of Gaza. Nothing is clear, no one knows what the future holds, and no one has any control over their fate.

Speaking of language, I have noticed that while writing my diaries, I use the phrases 'my home' and 'the place we are living at' to refer to the location of the host family. I keep reminding myself to use terms like 'the host family' and 'the place we are staying at temporarily'. Sometimes I wish I could slap myself in the face for not easily using those words and having to remind myself to do so. I want to go back to my street, to my home, to my bed.

Yesterday, Ahmad and I were out trying to find some long-sleeved undershirts for me so I could keep warm at night. We did not find any. In one street, he said: 'I don't know why, but I hate this street.' I remained silent. I hate the whole area we are staying in. It is true that they welcomed us, that we are 'safer' because we are here, but this area is a reminder of every horrible thing we have been through. But then I wonder, if we survive, won't everything and everybody around us be a reminder?

11 p.m. Two of my best friends left Gaza because some of their family members have dual nationality – another reminder of how cheap the lives of Gazans are. I told them to leave and never look back, not to think of us, and to think only of themselves and their children and their future. They left with little money and just a few items of clothing. They don't know what is waiting for them on the other side, but at least they know they will be safe.

After 2014, almost all of my close circle of friends left Gaza. They left their prestigious jobs and the lives they had been accustomed to. Apparently, they made the right decision. And now, the same thing is happening. My friends won't be back. This time, I was not even able to say goodbye to them, we were not even able to have one last cup of tea in one of our favourite places or a drive by the beach. I did not even get the chance to take one last photo with them or hug them.

I cry all night. I feel piles and piles of humiliation, injustice and dehumanisation.

I feel unheard. I am unheard.

Tuesday 21 November

8 a.m. A woman I know once wondered about what life would be like if tears were coloured, if there were a specific colour for tears of joy, sadness, anger, despair or helplessness.

We have reached a stage where it is not a surprise to see someone crying in the street. They might have lost someone, they might have lost their home, or maybe they have no place to go. The list could go on and on.

I leave early every day to start searching for anything useful. The shops open early to welcome all the lost souls. I call us the 'lost souls' because we don't know who we are any more. We had jobs, dreams and somewhat normal routines. Then suddenly we had to leave, and found ourselves in places we have never lived in before. Now, we are facing the unknown. Our minds and souls are lost.

I see a man bringing a big bag with *saj* bread. He starts calling out to let people know that he has something to sell. I run and reach him first. I ask him for some bread and pay him. Just like that. Then many people start running towards him. I take the bread – no, I *hug* the *saj* bread – and pass through the gathering crowd. I have a big smile on my face. For almost half an hour I keep walking, not focusing on where I am going. I'm just feeling happy.

A tear falls down my face. It does not need a colour. It is not a tear of sadness. We have reached a stage where getting bread easily is a victory, and it is a tear of gratefulness. I am grateful.

9 a.m. I pass by a small shop that sells purses and scarves, when a small scarf catches my attention. I have the same one. In fact, I have several, but in different colours in my home in Gaza City. I tie them over the handles of my luggage to mark them, after one time I bought a bag in the most unique colour of red. When the bags were coming out in the baggage claim, I saw at least five bags exactly the same, and since then, I have decided to be creative.

I go inside and buy one of the scarves, to give myself hope that I might travel again. The shop owner asks me which colour. I let him choose. He gives me the pink one. At home, I knot it around one of the 'escape bags' we have ready. Today, it is an escape bag; tomorrow it will be a travel bag, to a new destination.

11 a.m. I am walking with Ahmad, when we pass a bombed house. The house has collapsed and looks like a pile of giant Lego pieces. The surprising part is that there is one part of the house that is still perfectly fine – the kitchen and the room next to it on the second floor fell in one piece over the rubble. Even the kitchen sink is perfectly fine.

I stop for a while to look at the scene, and think of the owners and how they would feel every time they pass by. I bet there have been a lot of happy moments in that kitchen, cooking meals for family gatherings and maybe gossiping about what's happening. The next room could be a playroom for the children or maybe a teenager lying on their bed thinking of their crush. Then it hits me: did the residents of the house make it out alive? Or were they sleeping when it happened?

1 p.m. I am in the room when I hear the family outside talking. It seems that the oldest granddaughter has been suffering from a terrible toothache, and no painkiller is helping. It is good that they had painkillers, because I have noticed that pharmacists give the customers only one or two pills to ensure they have some left for anyone else in need.

'No clinics are working,' her father is saying to her mother. 'There are no doctors working these days. What should we do?' I feel very sorry for the girl and her parents, who can't help her, and I cannot stop thinking about the many children with more serious problems whose parents cannot help reduce their pain.

Then I remember, when I was at one of the shops, I saw a piece of paper stuck to its entrance. It said that in urgent cases of tooth pain, a doctor is available. I took a photo of it, so I check my phone and give the father the number. He is surprised: how is it that the newcomer, who has never lived in this area before, knows about it? I tell him it is an intensive course – I am spending hours every day going back and forth, checking shops, street vendors and any other place for resources to survive. So it has become normal to know this information.

He calls the doctor. He and Ahmad come back later and tell us that the doctor took out one of her teeth. He prescribed a certain medicine that they luckily found in one of the pharmacies. I ask her if it was painful; she shakes her head. I feel happy that she is OK.

3 p.m. I go outside again, and I meet a young man. We start chatting, and I learn that he has evacuated with his wife

173

from Gaza City. He tells me that he works as a marketing manager for a foreign company, and due to the current situation, he hasn't worked in over forty days.

He was surprised when the manager sent him his salary with additional money. He said that he felt shame for receiving money for work he hadn't done. The manager told him that his job will be secure no matter how long the war lasts.

I was glad to hear about such kindness. For a second, I wanted to take his phone number, maybe we could be friends one day, but then I decide: no, if it is meant to be, we will meet again in Gaza City, and we will be glad we both made it through this alive.

8 p.m. Our host family surprises me. Despite all the miserable things, and the daily struggle to secure bread, drinking water and water for toilets and washing, the struggle of dealing with fear, stress and uncertainty, they manage to gather – grandparents, children, the wife of the oldest and three grandchildren – and for an hour or two at night they talk, laugh and sometimes sing and play games.

They always invite me and my sister to join them, but we politely refuse. We want to ensure we don't invade their privacy, especially now that the whole evacuation situation has gone on much longer than we anticipated.

I don't know how to describe it, but they are people of simple dreams and simple lives. I admire how they manage to tune out all the distraction and fear for a short while to enjoy being a family.

11 p.m. Lying on the couch reflecting on my day, I am glad that amid all the misery, there is still space for acts of kindness, signs of hope and moments of joy.

I believe that hope is an inner feeling, but from time to time, it should be a decision. And tonight, I choose to be hopeful. I close my eyes to try to relax, and I hope for a better tomorrow.

Thursday 23 November

8 a.m. The grandchildren of the host family 'partially' adopted a cat. He is a big cat that was clearly a pet. I can tell he was raised in a home with land; he has all the features of a pet cat, but he can manage being outside as well. The only challenge is that their mother is terrified of cats, an additional reason we never let ours outside the room we are in.

The cat is allowed to stay in the small space between the two sets of stairs. They gave him a fluffy mat and offer him food there. Most of the time he stays at the entrance of the home, and sometimes, mainly in the morning when their mother is in the kitchen, they sneak him inside to play with him. It saddens me that he doesn't have better living conditions, but taking into consideration the situation we are going through, this is very good.

The kids come into our room to ask for food for their cat. We have a quick chat. The oldest girl says her mother 'has no job'. I try my best to explain the concept of 'unpaid labour' and that what their mother is doing is as important, or even more important, as what their father does outside the home. We talk for ten minutes, and then I realise that we might not even live to see another day. So I decide to end the lecture.

On their way out, I feel a little guilty for closing this opportunity to spread awareness, so I quickly tell them, while one of them is holding the doorknob, the other holding the food can and the third looking outside: 'And by the way, women can achieve anything they want. They can be the managers and leaders of the biggest associations, or, if they choose to, they can be housewives.

'Men can cry, wear pink, express their feelings and they can grow their hair long, and they can be stay-at-home dads, if they want to. It is OK for a woman to be a mechanic and a man to be a beautician.'

They gave me a look that says: 'Can we leave now? We have a cat to feed.' I let them go.

In fact, our hosts are gender pioneers. Ahmad has a sister who is studying abroad. In the neighbourhood they are living in, no girl has ever travelled abroad by herself to study. When she was about to travel, uncles came to their house and yelled at her father for the 'horrible thing you are about to let your daughter do', and said they would never talk to him again. Even neighbours shared their disapproval of such a move happening.

However, the grandmother discussed it with her three sons. They all agreed to support their sister. They went to their father and told him they were willing to face the stigma from the community. The sister travelled to study, and since then, she has been an inspiration. Later, two other families sent their daughters to study abroad, and now they consider the sister as a focal point for female students there. After one year, the family repaired the relationship with the uncles.

11 a.m. I am arguing with a street seller over the price of plastic bags. These bags have been added to the list of luxury

items; when you go to buy anything, the sellers give you the product without a bag because either they don't have any or because of their high price.

I meet a guy I know. He tells me that nothing matters or scares him; the only thing he is concerned about is his wife. He tells me: 'My wife is eight months pregnant, and her pregnancy has been difficult since the beginning. I am terrified of the options. I hope this whole situation ends before she gives birth.'

I tell him that hopefully this will end soon, even though I am not sure at all. He remains silent, while I wave away flies over my head and double check, for the thousandth time, my phone and my wallet, to make sure they are safe. Losing them would be a nightmare.

Then he tells me: 'I read that women in Gaza are giving birth through C-section, without anaesthesia. This is one of the scariest things a woman could go through. If this happens to my wife, I don't know what I will do.'

I try to calm him, and we talk for a while. After we part ways, I remember a friend who once shared with me how difficult a C-section is, when I casually asked: 'Why don't all women have C-sections, since they will have anaesthesia and not feel the pain of natural childbirth?'

She explained that in a C-section, they cut seven layers of skin to reach the baby. She shared with me the pain after the surgery, saying: 'The first cough a woman has after a C-section is deadly. The pain is horrible.'

I really hope his wife gives birth with complete medical care.

178

4 p.m. Ahmad shared with me an incident that happened in front of him in the market that shook me to the core. A man was selling some blankets in the street. It goes without saying that the price he was asking for was much higher than normal. Another man came to him and asked him for the price, and then he bought all of them.

The other man took them to another spot nearby and began selling the blankets for 25 per cent more.

The misery of prices continues. If you bought an item yesterday, you cannot simply assume the price is the same the next day. One common phrase is: 'How much is it today?'

I am terrified of where we are heading.

7 p.m. The ceasefire.

All people have been talking about is the ceasefire that will happen tomorrow. My friends who have better access to the internet keep sending me updates. Everyone is anxious that anything might happen within the hours left before it goes through, which will hinder the whole thing.

Waiting and praying for a ceasefire to happen, people are still sad and exhausted. People are still displaced; homes and complete areas ruined; many lost their loved ones; dreams were aborted; and the situation is miserable.

A guy told me a couple of days ago that he was tired of the daily survival attempts Gazans are going through. How every minute of the day is another struggle: for safety, for water, for internet, for clothes, for blankets – and to keep sane.

I hope, I really hope, a ceasefire will be the first step towards the end of this nightmare.

Friday 24 November

9 a.m. Ahmad is one of the most helpful people I know. He collected some money from friends and got a big tank of drinking water to take to where displaced families are located. He chose an area that has two schools full of evacuees. According to Ahmad, water is delivered to the schools, but some of them have more than ten thousand people inside. So no amount of water is enough.

The bottleneck was not getting the money; in fact, the money was the easiest part. For almost a week, he had been trying to reach the water provider, but couldn't. Even though the communication companies are working again, the service is very weak. If you need to call someone, you will have to dial them hundreds of times to have a chance of getting through.

I wonder about the lady chosen to record the message: 'The mobile number you have dialled cannot be reached at the moment.' Was she happy to be the voice of the company? Did she know that millions of Gazans cry after hearing her voice for the fiftieth time? Some of them even throw their mobiles aside in despair because they cannot reach their loved ones.

I wish she could say: 'I am sorry you cannot reach the person you are dialling. I hope you will be able to get to them soon. You are worried, and I know that.'

Eventually, Ahmad went to the house of the water provider and waited, on two consecutive days, to catch him.

I ask Ahmad if I can accompany him, and he agrees. We meet the man. He drives a small truck with the water tank on it. The water provider tells me that at five o'clock every morning, he goes to the sanitation station – the one that has drinking water – and waits for three to four hours for his turn. Then he comes back to start delivering the water. He said people think he does not want to help, but he is doing his best.

He tells me he is an excellent *dabka* dancer and says: 'Check TikTok for videos of weddings in the area, and you will see me dancing *dabka*. We love life, but we don't have the chance to live it.'

9.30 a.m. We reach the street where the schools are. The plan is to park outside in the street so people from the school and nearby homes can come and collect water. I am sitting in the seat next to the window. The situation is miserable.

I see many people holding their water containers and either standing in line to pay for them to be filled or on their way to go to a faraway place to fill them for free. When they see us arrive, they do not expect us to be stopping in their area, because usually the tank will be booked for a residential place.

Through the window of the truck I tell people holding the water containers: 'We are here to fill your water gallons for free.'

Suddenly, people start running towards the truck. The driver can't even move. Ahmad has to get out to ask them to give us space to park properly. People are screaming to others inside the schools: 'Come out and bring your gallons. There is free drinking water. Quickly!' And everyone runs.

In minutes, a very long line of men, women and children has formed, all with their water containers – names written on them to avoid losing them. If everything I had seen was not another reminder of how privileged I am, this is. Because for me, losing a water container is not a big deal; but for them, that simple item is critical. But many people bring buckets, empty cleaning-detergent containers, shampoo bottles and even plastic jars used for spices. A man helps the water provider organise the line.

Ahmad tells me that he wants to go inside one of the schools to check on his friend and his family that have evacuated there. I go with him. The school is no longer an educational entity; it is literally a camp. Tents are everywhere. There are 'boundaries' using carton, cloths and shop signs. Inside one of the classes, there are several sections; one of them is separated by some clothes used as curtains. A paper sign hangs, saying: 'There are women inside. Please give a warning before you move the curtains.'

A man is sleeping on a mattress in what used to be the playground. He is not in a tent or anything. A guy approaches him and tells him about the water truck outside. He asks: 'So, how much is water today?' When he learns it is free, he runs barefoot to secure a spot in the line.

A while later, we go outside to check on progress. A girl, about fifteen years old, wearing prayer clothes, gets out of the line after filling the jug she has. She can't even wait to use something to put the water in. She takes off the lid and drinks the water. She closes her eyes to enjoy it. She puts the lid back and goes back towards the school with a big smile on her face.

10 p.m. I receive photos from two amazing people. Both photos are of me with friends at a spot by Gaza beach, next to a sign saying: 'I love Gaza.'

I look at the beautiful pictures. That is the Gaza I remember, the one full of hope and beauty – not the one of women, children and men waiting in line to get a gallon of water. I look at the pictures and I don't recognise myself any more.

I really miss Gaza.

Sunday 26 November

3 a.m. Manara starts meowing loudly all the time, while rolling on the ground and arching her back. At first, we doubted she was in season, but the vet confirmed it. As a result, we can't sleep – one of the most important things we are looking for in a ceasefire.

Everyone hopes the ceasefire will be the first step towards ending the whole situation. For us, the ones who have already evacuated, the main difference is the lack of planes all day, walking without fear of being bombed, the ability to stay out till later in the night. And – for those who don't have cats in heat – sleeping. I have also noticed that a lot of married women have a chance to visit their parents, as most couples stay with the husbands' parents.

But fear and sadness still dominate. For many Gazans, this is a break from death. The most important question is: what will happen after the ceasefire? Our lives will move to being in danger immediately. Via the internet, many people have connected with others who fled from their neighbourhoods, sharing news about losing their homes and loved ones.

I hear a discussion happening outside among members of the host family. At 3 a.m. yesterday, Ahmad and his older brother left with two cooking gas canisters to secure an early spot to refill them. Filling gas is the top priority for almost every Gazan family during the ceasefire. They waited for over fourteen hours but couldn't fill them. The discussion today is about whether to go or not. They decide not to. I hear them talk about how undignified the whole situation is, and how they can depend on burning wood, hoping the situation will end soon.

During the ceasefire, there were sighs of relief, but also a lot of misery, tears and fear.

9 a.m. While walking in the street, I run into a friend of mine, a father of three adorable children. He is with his eldest child, who is wearing Mickey Mouse pyjamas and yellow Crocs.

My friend told me that he and his parents and brothers' families fled together. Due to their large group, they divided into two: women and men. The women stayed at a small apartment of a friend of his, and the men stayed at a cafe metres away.

A huge bomb landed nearby. It was very close to the women's apartment. He says it was the worst night in his whole life. 'We couldn't see anything – it was night, and the atmosphere was full of dust. When we reached them, barefoot, all we could hear were the women's screams.

'I thought someone had died. I thought my kids had died. But thankfully they were safe. A big door fell over my mother – now she cannot move her left hand. Afterwards, I noticed that my wife was repeating one movement at the same rhythm, as if clapping, but without her hands touching. I asked her to stop, but she cannot.'

We chat for a while, and he tells me: 'I can somehow handle everything we are going through, but the suffering of my children is unbearable. They are always terrified; they are away from their home and they don't understand why.'

An hour later, I see a young lady I know. She and her mother are visiting relatives who fled to the area we are staying in. We start checking on our mutual friends. When I ask her about someone, she says: 'She is having the best days! She and her family fled to the same house that the guy she is in love with fled to with his.

'During the period, the families got really close to each other, and the relationship became official and approved by everyone. Every time I talk to her, she shares the struggle and fear they are going through, but a part of her is full of love.'

At the vegetables stand, I meet a woman, the owner of an embroidery shop I used to buy products from all the time with my friends. She introduces me to her husband.

'It is confirmed now,' she tells me. 'We lost our home and our shop. I am terribly sad, but this is something to deal with after this is all over. My concern now is my only daughter; she refuses to eat and she got sick. We are staying with almost sixty people in a small space.'

9 p.m. My friend sent via SMS a post she read. A woman finally got the chance to visit her family, who fled to another area. Her nephew has taken Spider-Man as an imaginary friend, and he would always share their adventures with her. When she saw him, she asked him how Spider-Man was doing.

'He was killed.'

'How?'

'His house was bombed.'

186

I often get asked the question of: 'Do you think about marriage?' The older I get, the more decisive I become about not wanting to get married in Gaza. If there is one thing I want, it is for my children to have a healthy life, to enjoy riding a bicycle, and to have alive imaginary friends who have stories with happy endings.

I want my children to fall in love at school or university or doing theatre; not under bombing and amid a struggle to find food and water. I want my kids to live in a home that gets redecorated to become more beautiful; not a home that gets bombed and ruined. I want my kids to eat good food and to have the normal life that all children deserve.

Wednesday 29 November

9 a.m. When I was young, whenever my father travelled he would come back with a small suitcase filled with bottles of perfume. It did not take me long to realise my passion for perfumes and essences. I never believed that perfume is an accessory or a hygiene item; instead, it is a part of your personality and identity. No perfume is good for all; what is good on you could be horrible on another. The only exception is Chanel No. 5; it fits every woman on Earth.

A trip to buy perfume is a fun ride for me. I enjoy comparing the different essences and the ones that fit my current mood or state. I never get out of a perfume shop with fewer than three bottles, even if I don't need any.

I was talking with my friend over the phone. It has been almost two months since our lives were turned upside down. After going through the regular talk about the lack of food, water, internet connection and our fear of the future, she tells me: 'I know it is silly, but I have to confess, I miss my mugs and notebooks. You know that I have a huge collection. When we fled our home and evacuated, I never thought it would be this long. I only took the essentials. Now, after two months, I realise that my mugs and notebooks should have been among those essentials. Does this make me a shallow person?'

I told her that her feeling just makes her a human being who misses a part of her own self. Just like a puzzle, while some parts are essential, like staying alive in our case, some are small pieces but important to complete the whole.

I, too, left thinking I will go back in a couple of days. I miss a lot of 'unnecessary' items. I miss the night lamp next to my bed that I used to read before I went to sleep. It took me a while to choose the perfect one. I miss my childhood photos that are kept in a small box in my drawer. And I miss my perfume bottles; I miss them a lot.

2 p.m. The building belonging to the second family we evacuated to is destroyed. I heard the news from my sister after getting back from a failed hours-long search for cheese. Since the ceasefire started, people have been getting access to others, who told them, or shared pictures and videos, about the status of their own homes and their loved ones. This was the family we were with when the announcement of the evacuation south came.

This is the family we sat with at the table and with whom we had one of the most difficult conversations in our lives about whether we should leave or stay. I still remember the moment the wife stood and said: 'I have a feeling that if I leave, I am never coming back.' Her feeling was true; even if this whole nightmare ends, she will never go back to her house.

When I heard the news, I couldn't control the tears. It is never the same when it is someone you know. I can never imagine that the family that hosted us, and provided us with a safe place, lost theirs for ever. I know how every member worked hard on every single detail of both apartments in the building they were in.

I calm myself down and send SMS messages to all of them. Due to the bad communication network, I haven't been able to call any of them, and for the last couple of days we have been communicating only via SMS.

I wish I were there with them, to hug them and to give them a shoulder to cry on.

4 p.m. My back is killing me. I am not sure whether it is because I have been sleeping on a couch for almost two months or because of the continual crouching in the middle of streets, or because of holding heavy items and walking for hours. One thing I am sure of is that the stress and tension my body has been going through are the main reasons for the horrible pain I have been having. I decide to get medicine from the pharmacy.

On my way, I see a carriage pulled by a donkey with about ten people in it. Since the whole situation started, and with the lack of fuel, the carriages led by donkeys and horses have become the main method of transport. It is horrible and inhumane. Not only for the people, but for the poor animals who have to pull them.

I see a boy, a neighbour of the family we are staying with. He knows we have cats, so he asks me if we can take another one. I tell him that right now we don't have space for a new one, and I ask him for the reason. He says that a twelve-year-old friend of his, who evacuated with his family from the north of Gaza, is staying in a tent.

'He is looking for someone to take his cat. The life in the tent is very bad; they cannot take care of themselves. He is very sad, but he decided to choose what is best for the cat and let him go.' He says he will keep looking to find a safe space for the cat.

I reach the pharmacy and see a woman I know with her daughter. They are buying medicine for knee pain. I assume the mother is sick, but her daughter, twenty-three, was having horrible knee pain as well. 'I have been sleeping on a mattress on the ground for two months, and the weather is cold. My knees hurt me a lot.'

8 p.m. Not surprisingly, the continual checking is growing less. My friends who used to call several times during the day now call once every couple of days. Those who were glued to the screens watching the news are now focusing more on their everyday lives.

This nightmare has been going on for two months, and I am sure that they, too, are drained, in their own way, by the whole situation. Even I try to distract myself from the reality whenever possible. It is just sad and scary. People think that being in a ceasefire is a festive thing; they don't realise the burden and agony we are still going through.

There is an Egyptian proverb that says: 'Like those who danced on the stairs: neither seen by those above nor those below.' I wonder, are we Gazans the ones dancing on the stairs? No one saw or heard us dancing and building happy memories and lives, no one saw us planting flowers and achieving dreams, no one heard us singing and ululating during weddings and other happy occasions. And, right now, no one is seeing us dying every moment, crying for help.

I turn on music and listen to a piece by the Arab musician Omar Khairat. It's called 'Mrs Hickmat's Conscience' and refers to an old TV show with the same name. The small cat decides to sit on my belly and listen with me. I close my eyes and think of Gaza beach, the delicious breakfasts I had with my friends, the night lamp I had next to my bed, my childhood photos and my perfume bottles.

Friday 1 December

4 p.m. Dear Santa,

Every year around the first days of December, we put our Christmas tree in its spot and decorate it. Our cats love staying under the tree and playing with the big decoration balls and ornaments. The tree stays until mid-January, until my sister decides it is time to put it away. She says it is to 'keep the Christmas joy and spirit, and to feel happy every year'. I am Muslim. Muslims in Gaza love Christmas. Christians and Muslims gather every year to light up a huge Christmas tree in the YMCA centre to celebrate the happy occasion.

I am not sure you received the updated lists of Gazan children, but this year, many children in Gaza are dead. No, Santa, they were not naughty. Angelina Jolie once gave a speech about how difficult it is for her to understand how another woman, who is way more talented than her and has the ability to make better films, is located in a refugee camp, unable to find food for her children, and has no voice. Just like that woman, the Gazan children's only fault was where they were born: in Gaza, facing death, every single minute.

I read once that 'the soul is healed by being with children'. Not our children, Santa. Our souls are aching because of being with them. Yesterday, over the phone with my friend, who is a mother of two adorable children, she told me that I am lucky not to have any. 'My kids are sad all the time, they are cold and they are scared. My son told me he wishes to eat his favourite chocolate one more time before he dies.'

But her children are lucky because they found a shelter over their heads. Many children are in tents during these very cold times; some of them have poor parents who cannot afford to get anything for them. In the past days we had a ceasefire, and we were relieved for a while, but now it is over and the situation is very difficult. Nobody is safe.

This year, if you come to Gaza, and please do, would you change the gifts you bring? I know that you and the elves work all year to prepare them, but the priorities have changed. Don't bring dolls and bicycles to the children. Instead, bring some blankets, because they are cold. And although I love my friend's son, don't bring him his favourite chocolate; bring some food and flour, because children in Gaza are hungry.

Also, can you bring an insulin shot for the woman who has a diabetic son and is seeking one at any price? Can you bring with you milk for our friend's two-year-old daughter? Can you bottle safety and hope and bring them to our children? And, if any is left, to us, the adults, too?

You will not see Christmas trees, not because children stopped believing in or welcoming you, but because the trees have been burned as wood to stay warm at night. And there will be no chimneys, so please, look for the schools where thousands are displaced. Look for the tents, there are children in there.

Santa, if you come to Gaza, you will not recognise it. Buildings are gone and places that witnessed happy occasions no longer exist. There is no electricity. Recently, I have been remembering a quote I read years ago in a book entitled

The Perks of Being a Wallflower: 'This one moment when you know you're not a sad story. You are alive. And you stand up and see the lights on the buildings and everything that makes you wonder.'

Will you believe me if I told you that seeing lights over buildings is equal to realising that I am alive? My friend told me that her biggest dream is for someone to call her, and she can say, casually: 'I am doing nothing. I am just at my home, chilling.'

This year, everything is being tested: our survival skills, our patience, our faith and our humanity. We are exhausted, terrified and not sure if we will survive. Death is everywhere around us; we don't have the ability to cry over our loved ones, to hug them one last time or to grieve.

Maya Angelou said: 'There is no greater agony than bearing an untold story inside you.'

The amount of feelings and experiences bottled inside my head, heart and soul could fill this whole world we are living in. Can you imagine the agony all Gazan children, mothers and fathers have right now? How many have already died without even sharing their dreams with the world? How many have lost their futures without having a fair chance to achieve them?

Days ago, I was with the son of the host family we evacuated to. We heard about a man who sells wood, so we walked for over an hour to reach him. Since there are no containers or bags to put the wood in, he tied the pieces with a wire to keep them together. On our way, it started raining heavily. The evacuating people, looking for necessities, still wearing summer clothes, were shivering. All of us stood by the side of the road to wait for the rain to be over.

I looked at the boy and told him that I believe in the power of prayer, especially during rain. I asked him to pray for something. Santa, he did not pray for the game he had spoken about for almost an hour with me, nor did he ask for clothes. He said that he prays this whole nightmare will be over, and that he and his siblings will be safe.

I wonder, by 25 December, will this be over? Will I be alive, will I gather with my friends, exchange gifts and sing together 'Jingle Bells'?

Sending you love,
from Gaza.

Thursday 7 December

2 a.m. Wide awake, I am trying to understand the feeling or state I am in. One thing I know for sure is that it's not the first time I have had this feeling; I know I have had it once before. One time only. But I cannot tell when.

Two months have passed; just when you think you have reached the worst point, you get surprised by a new low. The last three days have been unimaginable. Many of the people who fled their houses once and twice and three times had to flee again. There are no places left. Complete families are in the streets. Women and children are there, with nothing to protect them. My friend, who, till this moment, couldn't believe how fast things had moved, tells me: 'We are like animals now, in the wild. I am terrified for my newborn child.'

It could be anyone, any time. Everyone keeps asking about places to host them or their loved ones, knowing very well the answer.

The closed shops are scary. They had previously been almost empty, but they were open, with a non-essential product or two. Now, they are shut. There is nothing left. Street sellers who have an item or two are asking crazy prices. These days, even money has no value. You have money, yet you cannot buy anything. Also, everyone is sick. Fever and flu due to lack of proper housing conditions; backache due to carrying heavy stuff and being sat in awkward positions while waiting in lines; stomach ache due to the unsanitary food and lack of healthy water.

I am trying to figure out the feeling I have got. I know I have had it before. Suddenly, I remember. It was years ago, when I saw a photo. A photo of a Sudanese child during a famine. He or she was on the ground, unable to walk due to exhaustion, and a vulture was waiting, very close, for death so it could eat.

That is how I feel. On the ground, unable to move, my face down. The emptiness inside me; the weakness and helplessness. All unbearable. There is no energy left to hope. Despite all the chaos around me, there is horrible silence inside my heart and soul. It feels like a desert, nothing visible, waiting for death, silently.

2.30 a.m. The members of the second family we fled to, the ones who discovered recently that their house had been destroyed, were able to leave Gaza. As holders of dual-nationality passports, their names were approved over a month ago. Yet they refused to leave at first and wanted to stay. Then they reached a stage where there was nothing left for them. They had no options. They left.

I think of them and the others who left. I think of their last messages while they were in Gaza. Apologetic ones saying they feel as if they are betraying the rest of the Gazans and letting them down by leaving. Despite their misery, they still feel horrible for leaving, for having a chance at being alive. Some of them were crying, some of them were talking in a hurry. I remember telling every single one of them to leave and never look back, to save themselves.

A couple of friends called me from Egypt a day or two after they arrived. They sounded completely different. They sounded like normal people who had a good night's sleep, who are not talking while worrying they might be bombed at any minute. They sounded like people who have had a good meal, of their own choice, and maybe they had some dessert, too. Instead of referring to all of us collectively as 'we', they have started referring to us as 'you', and to themselves as 'we'.

Right now, everyone is so lacking in hope that they don't wish the situation to be over, they just wish that they or everyone will be able to leave Gaza.

3 a.m. Manara is getting in a frenzy over mating. It has been almost two weeks she has been on heat, on and off, mostly on. We never thought it could last this long. The vet closed his clinic because it is not safe any more. We thought she might be in pain, stomach pain, but we realised we were wrong after Simba showed up.

Simba is a cat that my sister found in the street, lost. He was in good shape, but unfortunately some kids had cut his whiskers. My sister brought him and put him in the land next to us. He found his way and stayed with the other 'semi-adopted' cat that the host family's children keep at the doorstep.

My sister wanted to clean him, so she brought him into our room. Once he entered, Manara stopped meowing, she was very calm. Then, within a few minutes, she approached him, and they kissed. A while later, he grabbed her neck and was on top of her. We had to separate them immediately. If this nightmare continues for an additional month or two, we cannot take care of a pregnant cat or its kittens. We are not sure we will have enough food, or whether we will stay in our place and not be evacuated for a fourth time. This time, we will end up in the streets.

Manara's tail has been up recently, a sign of satisfaction or good health; she has been eating and drinking well. But her constant meowing is driving us crazy. Knowing there are two eligible males at the doorstep, she keeps meowing hard, all night, and they keep meowing back. My sister and I take turns calming her down. It is draining.

3.30 a.m. While holding Manara, I remember a conversation that happened outside our room between the host family members. There was no wood left to burn to prepare food, and it was not safe to go out and search for it, or even buy it, if that were possible. They decided to take out one of the wooden doors they have in order to cut it up and burn it. I heard their conversation, and argument, about which door should be taken.

Inside the room we are staying in, we have other debates. Another arrangement of 'escape bags' and discussions about what to take and what to leave. I go through my certificates and legal documents. I choose the most important ones and put them in the bag. The others I leave in another bag that we will leave behind if something bad happens. Even the weight of paper matters when running for your life.

Another debate, and guilt process, is the amount of food we eat. Every time we want to eat something, we have this feeling of should I eat it all? Should I keep some for later?

Should I give my portion to another family member? We are lucky enough to have food left; there are families out there with nothing to eat.

4 a.m. My throat is dry and my voice is very weak. Yet I choose to hum a Syrian song:

> *Take me to any country, leave me there, and forget all about me.*
> *Throw me in the middle of the sea, don't look back, I have no other option.*
> *I am not leaving for fun, neither for a change of scenery.*
> *My house was bombed and destroyed; and the dust of rubble blinded me.*
> *Let me try, no matter what, I am a human being.*
> *Call it displacement or immigration . . . just forget about me.*

Friday 8 December

2 a.m. My exhausted brain refuses to stop thinking about all the bad scenarios that I, my loved ones and all Gazans face if this nightmare does not end soon. I got brief and temporary access to the internet, and I unintentionally saw videos and photos of horrible things Gazans are going through. They made me realise that death could be a merciful fate. Awake and terrified, I knew it was going to be another long night.

The people in the next house seem to have had a long night, too. Their child did not stop crying for one minute. Yesterday, I was on a call with my friend. His wife, a doctor, gave birth to their third child, whom he described as 'healthy, beautiful, yet a very loud crier'. He tells me that now begins a new journey of finding everything a baby needs. 'In our house, the one we evacuated from, we had many items of the older children,' he told me. 'Also, my wife started preparing for the needs of the new one. We had to leave everything behind.'

There was an additional problem, he tells me. 'Can you imagine that right now I have no legal proof that my son is actually my son?' he says. 'My wife gave birth, and the doctor gave us a signed paper that said she did so, but there is nothing else to prove that this boy is ours. What if we get the chance to leave Gaza to save our lives? They won't let us take the boy.'

On a different note, he tells me that he filled his gas canister, which usually costs $17 to fill, for $157. To be honest, he sounded happier about the canister than the arrival of his baby. He was lucky because he was able to find a place to fill the canister and had money to do so. Our host family have been tirelessly working on filling a gas canister, but in vain.

Next to me is my sister, trying to calm the cat Manara down. Manara has fallen into a frenzy; her heat period has lasted over two weeks and is driving all of us crazy. Sleepless nights, continuous loud meowing, and now she's become aggressive. Minutes ago, my sister was patting her, when she scratched her, right under her eye. The eye swelled and it was very painful. Also, Manara has started peeing outside the litter box.

We have been trying everything we can. We consulted with one vet in person and several others by phone, which is never easy due to the horrible connection and the horrible period everyone is going through, including the vets. We talked to our friends who have cats. We reached a decision: we need to let her go mate and later handle the consequences of her getting pregnant, hoping the whole situation will end before she gives birth, if she decides to come back to us.

9 a.m. We say goodbye to Manara, who is meowing aggressively, and open the door for her. She goes out immediately, and Simba follows her. Simba is the cat who lost his whiskers and is staying on the doorstep. In no time, they start mating on the stairs, and when they finish she goes downstairs and he follows her.

When we get back to the room, my sister starts crying: 'I will miss her. She became a member of the family. The only reason I let her go is because I don't want her to suffer.

Our friends are leaving, our memories are erased, and now Manara has left.'

I completely understand. We don't have the energy for another loss. The only loss we try to focus on is the loss of our lives and how to stay alive in these horrendous days.

Manara and Simba remain around the house, on the land next to the neighbour's garage. We keep checking on them. Through the garage door, which is see-through (the door is like those of prison cells, with metal rods), we see her sitting on a plastic chair, sleeping. Simba is on the floor, next to the chair, just staring at her. She seems relaxed, and we are happy for her.

10 a.m. I go to the pharmacy to get medicine for my sister and to search for medicine for a friend of ours who has been desperately looking for some for her sick, elderly father. On my way, I wipe my nose with my hands, which, these days, is no longer impolite.

There are no tissues left. From time to time, you see someone selling pieces of cloth, similar to tissues, that can be used once, for a high price. Everything is scarce and needed. Even nylon trash bags, plastic wraps or anything else that can be found is being used for making fire to cook with and stay warm.

I reach the pharmacy and see a familiar scenario: a woman asking for lice medicine for her children. It is no surprise that lack of hygiene and showering while staying at schools could lead to such a problem. The pharmacist tells her no medicine is left, but there is a soap for lice that he might have somewhere. The mother has never heard of a soap for lice, but she has no other option, so she waits while he checks.

On my way out, I notice that the area in front of the pharmacy is now filled with many tents, made of cloth and fabric, with many families in view. I am stunned and I wonder how I haven't noticed this sudden change. The pharmacist tells me that every day people come and search for any area to stay in. 'They no longer ask for a house or even a covered space because they know it is impossible. Now, all they want is a space. Only a space.'

7 p.m. These days, I am afraid of checking my phone. Checking SMS messages is the toughest: either someone is dead, someone's house is destroyed, someone is in dire need of something essential or someone is missing.

I remember a day, before, when I had an important interview. I decided to wear a tie to look formal, but I don't know how to tie one. So I went to a friend's workplace to ask him for help. He showed complete support. But he, too, did not know how to do it. We opened a YouTube video, and he started following the instructions. People in the surrounding offices and visitors looked at us weirdly. After many failed attempts, and with the time of the interview approaching, he looked at me, gave me a big smile and said: 'Who said you need to wear a tie to impress a bunch of senior management people? You are charismatic and you have all that it takes. No need for the tie.'

We laughed, and I left his office, holding the tie in my hand. Then he called after me. I turned around, and he said:

'But I promise to learn how to do it before you get married. You need to look good in the pictures.'

When I received the message that my friend got killed, along with other family members, I turned off my phone. I don't know why, I just thought this will make it as if it did not happen at all. I continued doing what I was doing. Then I turned the mobile on, opened the message, read it and sat silently, trying to absorb the news.

He was a father of adorable children. He was loved by everyone around him. He was helpful, optimistic, inspirational and full of life. Now, he is no longer with us.

How many people will die before this is over?

Wednesday 13 December

8 a.m. I have never been a fan of the sun nor the sunny weather. I am a lover of the rain, winter and tree leaves falling. I remember at high school – my English language teacher would always ask me and other students during the recess to stand in the sun. 'Hug the sun, feel its warmth. It is full of vitamin D.' I did what she asked but never liked it.

On the other hand, this teacher opened the door for me to learn about literature, which I loved. In class, we would read summarised classics like *Great Expectations*, *Pride and Prejudice* and *A Tale of Two Cities*.

My friend shares with me the results of the Booker Prize; it seems that *Prophet Song* won this year. Based on brief descriptions of the shortlisted books, I see myself more interested in reading *The Bee Sting*.

I just wish to go back to spending a whole day in my bed, while it is raining outside, and enjoy reading one book after another. One fear I had was dying before reading enough of all the beautiful and great books in this world. Now, I am terrified of dying before even living my life.

But during these times, I cannot pray enough for the weather to be sunny. First, for those who are living in schools and tents not to suffer, and to be able to charge our batteries and phones using the solar power of our neighbours. Unfortunately, since yesterday, it has been raining heavily. We had hail. In no time, most of the streets around us were covered by water due to the poor infrastructure. Most people are still wearing flip-flops; shoes are a luxury they cannot afford. I have noticed many people wearing torn flip-flops. How can they move in the streets?

And what about food? Usually, people eat more to maintain the warmth of their body. But the opposite is happening. One friend of mine, who is average weight, told me that he has lost over 8kg (1st 3lb) so far. There is very little food available, yet they exert a lot of effort trying to secure basics. He tells me: 'You know what we did to reduce our suffering? The whole family decided to start fasting. This obligates all of us to not ask or wonder about food all day long. When the sun goes down, we have our only meal, depending on what is available.'

Many families have no access to flour, so they cannot even have bread. A friend, in another area, tells me: 'We haven't had a piece of bread in four days. We have children, which worsens our misery. We have some food left, but it is not enough. Adult men are crying in the streets begging to buy flour.'

Ahmad's younger brother comes into the room to say good morning. We discuss how sad we are to have such cold weather. He also discusses another luxury we no longer have: hot drinks whenever we want. Nowadays, with the lack of cooking gas, drinking something hot is a long process that starts with creating heat by burning wood or nylon, cartons and plastic. Also, you always need to check now whether it is a priority to drink to maintain resources.

He shares with us the memory of the last cappuccino he had: 'It was hot and delicious. I really enjoyed it and could feel its taste in my mouth till now. What irritates me the most is that I remember not completing my cup because I was in a hurry. I drank half of it and then left, not knowing it would be my last time to drink cappuccino. Now, two months later, I would drink it till the last drop.'

3 p.m. Ahmad has volunteered to help the displaced children in the schools and other areas. He goes with a group of youths and plays games with the children and their parents; he tells them stories and they sing together. He goes every morning at 8 a.m. and gets back at around three. I asked him about how he feels about this. He says the situation is horrible. Every classroom has about seventy people, including at least thirty children. He couldn't comprehend how they were able to divide the small room to include four or five families. He says the playground is a camp itself. You cannot put your foot in. The overpowering smell of sewage is just awful.

'But the children and their parents enjoy the activities. One thing we did was face-painting. One girl wanted a yellow dog; the other wanted a butterfly; and a boy asked for the sun. Their parents are grateful that we are creating some moments of happiness during these miserable times.'

At the end of our discussion, he recalls a young boy he met: 'He told me that he misses his house in the north, and he wants to go back there to his happy life.' The boy's mother told Ahmad that he does not know that his home was destroyed. Heartbreaking.

6 p.m. Even though those who left Gaza are in a much better place and they are safer, they are still facing many challenges. For instance, one friend of mine left Gaza with her family with almost no money. Now, they are borrowing money from friends living abroad, and she told me that she is looking for a job. So they are safe, but need to survive on their own.

But the biggest misery is the fear for their loved ones and the feelings of guilt for leaving them behind. Another friend received the news of the death of her brother and other family members. She is devastated.

10 p.m. Lying on the couch, covered with blankets trying to get warm, I think of one of the best book introductions that I've read. It was Charles Dickens: 'It was the best of times, it was the worst of times, it was the age of wisdom, it was the age of foolishness, it was the epoch of belief, it was the epoch of incredulity, it was the season of Light, it was the season of Darkness, it was the spring of hope, it was the winter of despair.'

Sitting in darkness, in Gaza's winter of despair, I wonder how Gaza is going through the worst of times, and how accurate the description in Dickens's introduction is of the world's current state.

I pray for this nightmare to be over; I pray that our suffering and misery will end. But right now, what I wish for the most is for the cold weather to disappear, and for the sun to come up so Gazans can stand under it to warm their bodies, and their hearts and souls.

Saturday 16 December

9 a.m. 'Cheese! Congratulations.' Two words written by my friend on a small piece of paper inside a tiny nylon bag that contains two packs of cheese. Each is 250g.

Recently, my displaced friends and I have started helping each other to find necessary products. The challenge these days is that there is no specific place to find anything. You find underwear at a library; food in an electronics shop; and glue at a spice shop. As a result, my friends and I share our needs, and all of us search for all of them. We leave any 'treasure' we find at a pharmacy that is relatively close to all of us. When someone finds something for another person, he or she sends them an SMS. However, the communications were cut again, and no one could contact any other person. So I decided to go to the pharmacy in case someone had found something I was looking for. And I was right: my friend had found the cheese.

A couple of days ago, another friend was looking for Cerelac (it is the brand name, but it is a wheat and milk cereal for children). So, every time I passed by a pharmacy, I checked for him, and I kept my eyes open. It was raining heavily; the sewage water reached our ankles, and we couldn't avoid it. After half an hour of walking under the rain, I was able to buy an umbrella, but it was too late. I bought another one for my sister. However, the one I was using broke immediately due to the very strong wind. So I used the other.

After hours of walking and searching for several things, I passed by a pharmacy. I was holding the umbrella, soaking wet and breathing heavily. I stood outside and asked: 'Do you have Cerelac or any other alternative?' One pharmacist looked at the other, and they asked me in. They told me that they have a small amount that they sell only to their customers after it was cut from the market. He said: 'The desperation in your eyes, you soaking wet and the umbrella played in your favour.' They thought that I was a father looking for one pack for his child, and I did not correct them. They gave me one for its regular price, not a doubled or tripled one. Something extremely rare these days.

The list of items that we keep trying to find for each other is long; it includes medicine, flour, yeast, pet food, cat litter, clothes, coffee, etc. My friend who found cheese is looking for rice. I hope to find her some soon.

One thing I am unable to wrap my head around is how our lives turned around from having jobs and full lives to simply caring about mere survival and finding the basics. I wonder what else we will be looking for in the future.

10.30 a.m. I take the new cat to the vet. Yes, there is a new cat. I found him days ago. He is so tiny he fits into my palm. It was raining heavily. The only reason I realised there was a cat in the middle of the street next to the trash was his shaking. He was lying on his face and breathing fast. I went closer and sat on the pavement. I was like: 'Please, stand up and show me that you are a strong, healthy cat.' But he wasn't.

I held him in my hand and looked for something to put him inside, but couldn't see anything. I found a homewares store (it sells mugs, cups, plates, etc.). I went inside and bought a plastic food box. I also bought a knife to make a hole in the top for the cat to breathe.

He has been with us for four days. He wakes up every two hours, eats, poops and goes back to sleep. This cat is the first one I've seen who eats like the cats on cartoon TV shows. He makes a num-num-num sound, which is super-adorable. I took him to the vet because he got uncontrollable diarrhoea. My sister tried some remedies she knows have worked before, like boiled-rice water or boiled potato, but nothing worked. The doctor gave me medicine to give him twice a day. By the way, he weighs 345g (12oz).

The children of our host family ask my sister what name she will give him, but she said this time he will have no name, just 'the cat'. They even suggested to call him Jack, after the other injured cat we got in who died. We both refused. I tell her that I have a name for him, but I did not share it with her or anyone else. I am even shocked that I chose that name for him. Out of all the names, I chose that name!

Speaking of cats, Manara, the injured cat we took in who left to mate, came back. She comes every day in the morning, enters our room, drinks a lot, then eats wet and dry food. She rests, and sometimes sleeps, then she stands by the door to leave. Apparently, we have become her little motel.

1 p.m. I see a child crying in the middle of the street. His mother was doing her best to calm him down, but she looked worn out. I sympathise with her and all parents. I remember a phone call I had with a friend of mine recently. She and her family are now staying in a home with almost fifty other people. The men sleep downstairs and the women upstairs. When she hears that my sister and I are staying in a separate room, she jokes and says: 'Wow! A private room is like a five-star suite.'

Like all Gazans, they are exhausted by the challenge of securing water. She tells me: 'Last night, my seven-year-old son was sleeping downstairs with the men. My husband told me that he woke up in the middle of the night to use the toilet. He came back and woke his father up; he was crying and he started screaming, not caring about the other people trying to sleep. He told his father that there is no water, no tissues and the toilet is not clean.'

I listen, and then I tell her that her son did what all of us want to do at some point: he woke up in the middle of the night and cried because he couldn't fulfil one of his basic needs, which is using a clean bathroom.

My friend has lost her house, too. She did not cry, but all she said was: 'The future ahead of us is very scary.'

9 p.m. Lying on the couch, thinking about how there are no signs this nightmare will end any time soon, my sister asks me again about the name I chose for the cat.

'It is just a name, I don't know why on earth I chose it, but I did.'

'What is it?'

'Hope.'

Wednesday 20 December

8 a.m. A new family joined us. They say it is temporary, but I don't believe it. Over two months ago, when my sister and I evacuated for the third time, we thought it was temporary. It seems there is no end to our misery, it will just get worse. The family consists of a mother and her children – two teenage boys and one young girl. They are relatives of the host family. Them joining means even less space, less resources and more fear. But that is all OK. What scares me the most is all of us having to evacuate again. There is no place to go to.

I know many friends who had to distribute themselves over several places due to their big numbers or the fact that no single place can contain them. I saw a friend of mine in the street, who told me that a part of his family went to the schools, he joined his friends in a studio apartment, another part went to relatives, and a few had a tent in an open area. When I hear things like this, I wish that this is all part of a novel or a soap opera, because it cannot be true.

I ask him how they keep in touch during the horrible and continuous communication cuts. He says that they try to send messages from time to time, and when the communication is completely shut down, they just go and visit each other. They go on foot, without any coordination, which means that he could walk for an hour and then not find anyone in their place because they are out trying to secure flour, water or wood to burn for warmth and cooking.

'But we are fine,' he says. 'We are better than others. When I went to visit my family who are staying in a tent, I saw another family, who told me that the only thing they ate in the last three days was raw onions. They had no money and couldn't find any help.' I knew from him that he got them some food, which I am grateful for.

10 a.m. A tailor has opened his shop in the area. When I went there to mend my pants, I saw people asking him why he opened now, and not earlier. 'I only opened because I have no money left. I have children and grandchildren that need to eat. What is safety when you have no food?'

I noticed that when people come to him, they don't carry the pieces they want to fix, they are actually wearing them. Many people left their houses wearing summer clothes. The lucky ones were able to buy a couple of items, but many have no money to do so. And most of those who got things don't have the luxury to buy two blouses, for example, to wear one each day. A man took off his trousers and stood behind a curtain while the tailor fixed them. Another man took off his hoodie and sat in his undershirt to wait for it to be sewn.

While behind the curtain, the man with no trousers on was talking to his friend on the other side. He told him that he saw someone whose flip-flops were torn, and he connected the torn parts together using a nylon bag. He observed him and noticed that he does not pick his foot up while walking, he just rolls it on the ground to keep the torn pieces together. He went after him and offered him a little money, but the man refused. He said that there are other people who deserve it more. After much persuasion, he took the money.

216

An elderly man was waiting for his turn to fix his jacket. He was wearing a mask. I know that he is staying with his family at a school. 'Our biggest fear is the diseases,' he tells me. 'There are thousands of people in each school. If one has a virus, everyone else will have it. Everyone I know has flu, stomach pain, back pain and fever. No one is safe. I am an old man with high blood pressure and diabetes. My body cannot handle any more health problems.'

2 p.m. One thing that keeps happening is running into people I know who lived in the north and Gaza City more than I used to see them when we were all there. It seems now that all Gazans are cramped into a small space, so the possibility of us seeing each other is stronger. The theme song of *Orange Is the New Black* comes to my mind: 'The animals, the animals, trapped, trapped, trapped till the cage is full.' Well, considering the living situation (or is it the dying situation?), we are animals trapped in a cage, hoping to stay alive while facing death.

I meet a guy I worked with many years ago. He tells me that he and around fifty of his family are staying at his relatives' house. 'My sister's husband is wealthy, so when they evacuated the first time, they bought a lot of food and supplies. Then they were informed to evacuate from the new area. They ran very quickly and left all the food behind. The building was bombed. Now, they are with us, with no food, no supplies, and with money that almost has no value.'

4 p.m. I found fifteen pills of my medicine! I am so happy. This means I am covered for two weeks. But the question is: how many two-week periods do we still have to endure until this nightmare is over?

6 p.m. Ahmad tells me that he is trying to buy some clothes for a child he saw in one of the schools. He said his whole family died, and he has no other relatives left. The neighbours took him with them when they evacuated. He is four years old; no one told him what happened to his family. He told Ahmad that 'they will come back to pick me up'.

10 p.m. A previous colleague of mine believed strongly in the power of energy. She always said that we attract the energy we surround ourselves with. So she had several cards and pictures on her desk of what she wants to achieve in order to 'attract it'.

I look for a piece of paper, but can't find any. I get a small piece of carton and write on it: 'The nightmare is over. I survived; I am alive.'

Monday 25 December

8 a.m. Little Hope, the new cat that I found shivering next to a trash pile a while ago, is getting much better. He is eating, growing up and playing. After the last visit to the vet, it was confirmed that he has a hernia. We were told to feed him the bare minimum. It really hurts seeing him meowing and asking to eat, yet not getting any food. What is worse is that the other cats have access to dry food and more meals than him. But it is all for his own health.

I took him to the balcony to let the other cats eat. I thought about Gazans right now who don't have access to food, while others do. A friend of mine told me that every morning, two young boys who evacuated with their families from the north of Gaza would knock on their door. They don't ask for money or any material. All they ask for is two pieces of bread for them to eat. 'It breaks my heart,' my friend told me. 'Even when I asked them if they want thyme or cheese with it, they said plain bread would be fine. They come to our house every morning, and I give them any leftovers we have.'

Back to cats. Our room is becoming a haven for strays. A new cat has found her way to us. She is huge. She is white with black legs, black hair round her eyes in the shape of a mask, and a huge black spot on her back. I decided to call her Sunshine. Sunshine finds her way to the apartment every morning; she gets in and stands by our door and starts meowing. She has the thinnest voice ever. We open the door for her, she goes directly to the food bowl, eats and then leaves. Manara does the same these days, with the addition of staying the night as well. She waits for me to lie on the couch and curls up next to my feet.

But even the cats' food is scarce. The place we buy from told us that there is not a lot left. And if the quantity ends, there wouldn't be any cat food available.

My sister and I are among the lucky ones who do have access to some food. Every time I eat something – anything – I thank God for the blessing I have, yet I feel guilty. How come I have food while there is another displaced child with no access to it? How come? What kind of a world are we living in?

10 a.m. New areas were asked to evacuate. People who have evacuated once or several times before and 'settled' in new places were asked, again, to leave. But there are no spaces left. Last week, a new family joined us, and this week, another one did. The situation is getting worse and worse.

My sister's friend and her two daughters came to visit. They have been staying in a school for more than two months now. But after the evacuation announcement in their new area, most families there left, and they had no place to go to. They asked if it was possible to stay with us. But the host family apologised, simply because two new families are staying with us. The woman's eyes were full of tears when she was explaining how scared she was for her and her two daughters' lives. Finding an apartment is impossible right now. But we contacted everyone we knew to search for available places for them to put a tent.

I feel awful about them and am very worried for their safety. I talk to Ahmad, and he promises me he will do his best to help them. On his way out of the room, I hear him talking to himself: 'Today is their turn; in a few days, it will be ours.'

The misery continues. A guy I know is staying with his family in a friend's apartment. When they had to evacuate, the apartment was empty. But with the new evacuation process, the host family itself had to move in as well. 'We offered to leave immediately, but the host family members started crying and begged us not to. Now, there are sixty people in a three-room apartment.'

I just cannot believe that our utmost hope has become finding a space for a tent. This is inhumane.

2 p.m. I go to check on my friend, who has been hosted by the family of a friend of his. They welcome me and invite me inside. I sit down with my friend, his friend and the family.

Fifteen minutes into the conversation, during which we discussed the usual (the lack of food, our safety, our fear of the future, etc.), the father, a seventy-three-year-old man, started crying. 'This is not the Gaza that I know. This is not how I wanted to spend the final years of my life. There are tents everywhere. People are begging for money. We are terrified for our lives. This is the biggest test we have ever had.

'If I die,' he says, 'will I have a place to be buried in?'

His wife tells me about her neighbour, a cancer patient who hasn't had her medicine in a long while. Such stories are no longer surprising. Her son looks at her and says: 'Aren't we all dying, slowly?'

On my way out, the father, whom I have met for the first time, asks if he could hug me. I couldn't be happier. He feels like a father to me. I am grateful for his hug. I needed it.

5 p.m. The youngest brother of the host family comes into the room my sister and I are staying in.

'I have bad news,' he says.

I jump off the couch. 'What? Do we need to evacuate again?' I ask.

'No, no,' he says, while doing a movement with his hand that means 'calm down'. 'It is something else. It is about charging.'

Every morning, he would take the batteries, flashlights and power banks to charge at the neighbour's house, which has solar power. He would take our mobiles and laptops as well, but after one mobile went missing, we stopped sending them.

He explains: 'By mistake, someone took out the cable that had all our devices connected to it. As a result, nothing was charged.'

My sister and I remain silent. Another night in complete darkness.

9 p.m. It is Christmas today. In another country, far away from ours, there is a family celebrating. Their house is full of light; they are smiling, hugging each other out of love, sharing gifts and hoping for the best future.

Here, there is no Christmas. Instead, there are families living in complete darkness, sad, hugging each other out of fear, sharing prayers and hoping they will get out of this nightmare alive.

Friday 29 December

8 a.m. For the past three days, my sister and her friends have been out for hours, searching for a place for her friend and her two daughters, who had no place to go. Finding a space to set up a tent is almost impossible these days, with the increasing numbers of displaced families from the surrounding areas. After a lot of searching, they were able to find a spot for them.

It was important that it is a place near to people we know in case they need help. My sister talked to the neighbours in nearby buildings, and they promised to take good care of them. Also, they offered to let them in when they need to use the toilets.

When it was time to set up the tent, they found another family wanted the place. It took them hours of discussion until the space was divided between the two families. Another challenge was securing the wood, blankets and nylon for the tent. They bought some, and some was given by families who wanted to help.

The mother and daughters were terrified till the last minute. They had never stayed in a tent before. But there was no other way. They kept asking questions about safety and logistics. My sister and her friends were doing their best; the tent was set up and everyone helped. Hours later, the mother and daughters heard that a distant family member had agreed to host them in their house. They told my sister they will go there.

My sister told me: 'Literally minutes after they left, a new family showed up, looking for a place to stay after evacuating.

They couldn't believe that a tent was set up and ready for them. The wife cried.'

3.30 p.m. I was able to get a weak internet connection, and a series of WhatsApp messages in my building's group showed up. I found out that a relative of one of my neighbours had been able to go and check on our building. He said that the building is still standing, yet in a horrible situation.

The damage is severe, and it might take a year just to fix it to be able to stay there if we go back. All the glass is broken and everything is damaged. He also said that displaced people from other areas got into the apartments and took the clothes, mattresses and wooden items to survive and burn for warmth. They took anything edible.

We have a proverb that says: 'A loss is better in money than in souls' – meaning that as long as you are alive, any tangible loss is less awful. But I have to admit that this wasn't what I felt at that moment. I shared the news with my sister, who was devastated.

I couldn't stay in my place, I couldn't breathe well. I found myself going out and heading towards a friend of mine, who has evacuated to a family far from where we are staying. But I did not care.

I was walking so fast that I was surprised by the short time it took me to reach there. I found his relative downstairs and asked him to go call my friend. He came down and saw my face and knew something was wrong.

'Is everything OK? Are you OK?'

'I want to walk.'

We started walking. I told him everything that I'd heard, while tears were falling down from my eyes. People in the street looked at me without surprise. These days, it has become very usual to see people crying in the street; no one even needs to ask you about the reason. My friend did his best to calm me down.

In that hour, I grew twenty years older. My fast-paced steps turned into very slow ones. I was not able to breathe well. I could feel the skin over my face and body wilt like a sunflower that decided to give up after the sun disappeared and it was left in darkness for a very long time. I knew for sure at that moment that I will not be the same person again.

Yesterday, my sister showed Ahmad some photos and video from the apartment. She wanted to show him how small the cats were compared with now. When I saw them, my heart ached. I saw the tiles, I saw the walls, I saw the Christmas tree we put up, I saw the windows, the furniture and many other details.

After a while, I couldn't stop moving, so I forced myself to sit down. Right in the middle of the street. My friend, who was calming me down, sat next to me and started crying. He told me about the news of several family members of his dying; he told me about his parents and brothers, who stayed in the north, and after many days of trying to reach them he knew that they are still alive, yet suffering. His mother told him that they are OK, but when he talked to his young niece, she told him they haven't had drinking water in a very long time and there is little food left.

I tried to calm him down. I just can't comprehend the amount of misery we are surrounded by.

10 p.m. For the past almost three months, I have realised new depths and meanings of the different feelings.

It turns out that sadness is even sadder than we used to think it was. Grief has many more other aspects than we thought. Happiness is way more difficult to feel or achieve.

And there are various new feelings that till now I cannot even put a name to.

Right now, all I want is to get out of this alive. To survive.

Sunday 31 December

6 a.m. In my culture, we have a superstition that says if you get an itch on the bottom of your feet, then you will travel soon; an itch on your right hand, and you will shake hands with someone important; left hand, you will get money; your nose, you will hear bad news.

After another sleepless night, I look at my sister, who was telling me minutes ago how much she misses a good night's sleep, and I tell her: 'I have an itch on the bottom of my feet and on my left hand. Do you think I will travel soon and get money?'

She says: 'I think your body is telling you that you need to take a shower.'

We laugh. Hygiene remains a big challenge, especially bathing. Having a bath has become, in the last three months, a luxury few people have. Most of the time we depend on medical alcohol and wet wipes to clean our bodies. Both are very difficult to find, and when you do, they are expensive.

A couple of days ago, my sister's friend invited her to take a bath at her house. They heated some water for her and put it in a bucket – something we never thought any of us would do in our lives. My sister came back happy. But she told me: 'I forgot how to take a shower. Has it been this long?'

Speaking of hygiene, the list of challenges goes on and on. Laundry, for example. We have been manually cleaning clothes, when there is available water. Due to the number of people in the place we are in, there is laundry everywhere: in the normal places, like balconies, and in abnormal ones, like chairs in the middle of the hallway, or on laundry threads (threads that are hung from one side to the other) in the bedrooms.

I wonder when it will be the turn of our hearts to be cleaned.

7 a.m. My sister leaves to visit her friend. Both her cats stand behind the door and start meowing. Do they feel afraid she might not come back? Is it the sadness of loss?

Loss has become another companion in our days. We have reached a stage of not sharing our losses with the others because everyone is suffering. Sometimes it feels like a misery Olympics, with everyone in the group facing their own tragedy: someone lost a loved one; someone lost their home; someone lost their dream; and someone lost all three of them.

One time, I read a quote from a book called *The Five Wounds* – I haven't read the book, but I hope to do so one day. It says: 'This is death, then: a brief spot of light on earth extinguished, a rippling point of energy swept clear. A kiss, a song, the warm circle of a stranger's arms – these things and others – the whole crush of memory and hope, the constant babble of the mind, everything that composes a person – gone.'

Remembering this quote gave me the freedom to think of the small details I miss about everyone I love. I miss the freckles on the face of our neighbour's son, who had a smile big enough to make your day. I miss my friend and colleague's loud laughter that used to make our manager come to the office and ask what was happening, and we would feel embarrassed. I miss my other friend's wonderful sense of style. She would take care of every single detail, from head to toe. I wonder how she looks now, but I am sure she is managing to keep in style, even in the worst of times.

There are many details that make you who you are. I am not sure – if I make it out alive – if I will still possess what makes me, me. And I wonder: will I be there in the future, or will I be someone to be remembered in a diary or over a cup of tea by a friend after I am gone?

10 a.m. I go to the tailor to fix a jacket that belongs to a member of our host family. An old man comes in and gives the tailor a pair of boxer shorts. He wants him to make an 'inner pocket'. He says: 'I am staying in a tent, and I cannot guarantee the safety of any money, no matter how little I have. So I want it to put the money in it.'

Next to me is a man who shares his story with all of us: he had a shop in Gaza City, but now finds himself displaced with his family, with no money left. 'I am trying my best to earn some,' he says. 'One day, I go cut some wood to sell for people to burn for cooking and warmth. If we get some flour, I take some of it and make pastries to sell.

'Sometimes I and my children take the water gallons of people and go to a faraway place to fill them, and they pay us. We have no option. It is about day-to-day survival.'

He has brought two of his children with him. I ask the first one: 'What is your favourite colour?'

'White.'

'And your favourite food?'

His eyes brighten: '*Shawarma!* I haven't had *shawarma* in a very long time.'

We talk for a while about all the kinds of food we haven't had in almost three months, then I ask his younger brother: 'What do you want to be in the future?'

'I want to be in school.'

His father tells me he is supposed to be in the first grade next year; he really wanted the year to pass in order to go with his siblings to school. Then he says: 'Now, even the schools are gone.'

'And what else do you want to do?' I ask.

'I want to draw. In my home, we had a lot of drawing books and pens, pencils and colouring pens. Here, we don't have anything. I want to play with my toys, too.'

10 p.m. If it weren't for someone I met in the street, I wouldn't have realised that it is the final day of the year. Now, all days are the same – periods of time passing without any meaning, showing us how cheap our lives are.

Ahmad was in our room, checking on us, when I had this silly idea. I raised my hands as if I were holding a plate. I told him and my sister I was holding the imaginary cake of the New Year's Eve celebration, and asked them about their wishes.

They gave me a look of 'How stupid is this?', but then Ahmad started, with his very horrible singing voice, singing New Year songs. We sang along for a couple of minutes. He left us, and we went to sleep.

That is how my year ended: displaced, sick, sad, unsafe, with the loss of many people, possessions and memories, and terrible mental health. It also ended with some singing and an imaginary cake.

Sunday 7 January

5 a.m. A beautiful bond has been created between Hope, the cat we rescued from the street, and our own little cat. But the term 'little cat' does not apply any more because she has grown and looks huge compared with Hope. She has become like a mother to him: she cleans him, they play together and sleep next to each other. When she sits, he looks at her tail, takes the 'ready' position and then attacks. He loves to wrestle with her.

Since the vet recommended we shouldn't feed him a lot, we have been watching his food intake. We keep the lid of the dry-food Tupperware box on so he can't open it. I have noticed that our little cat would go there and move the lid away for him to eat. He is so small that his whole body gets inside the Tupperware. The good thing is, his health is much better; he even has hair on his legs, which he didn't have before. The bad thing is, having this many cats is a huge burden we're not sure we can handle, especially given that nearby areas are being asked to evacuate. The horror is for us to face the same fate. My sister and I have had to go through our stuff again and decide what to take in case we have to leave suddenly. Living in constant fear is a living hell.

But the little cat is not the only one who has grown attached to Hope. We have, too. He loves skin-to-skin contact. For example, he will come to me and pick at either my neck or the small space between the bottom of my trousers and the top of my socks where the skin is showing. He will hug that part and sleep for hours. Also, whenever I sit with my legs bent to one side, Hope will come and put his head over my knee and just look around and observe us.

A very tough decision faces us that we have been trying to avoid: he needs another place, because we don't have the capacity to take care of him. For a few days, I have been looking for someone to take him. We have agreed to provide this person with the food, the required medicine and pocket money for any additional needs. Unfortunately, even the owners of cats wish someone would take theirs because of the harsh conditions we are going through.

Finally, a friend of Ahmad tells me his cousin is willing to take Hope in. I tell him I need to visit and make sure that the place is suitable, and more importantly, that his cousin is a good person. It is not enough that he is willing to take care of Hope, I need to make sure he is a loving, caring guy. We agree to meet the next day.

10 a.m. On my way to see a friend, I notice two women and some children sitting on the pavement. It is no longer a surprise to see people in the street with no place to go. I feel terrible because they are homeless, and I wonder: aren't we all homeless right now? Many people have evacuated for the third or fourth time, and there is no space left for them to go.

When I meet my friend, I tell him about the two women, and we go to see if we can help. They tell us they couldn't even find a tent to stay in and they had no place to go. My friend decided to knock on the door of the nearest house. He talked to the owner and told him about the situation. After much discussion, the owner agreed to let them stay in the entrance leading to the house. I asked to talk to his wife to make sure there are women inside and the place is safe. She came, greeted us and said they would provide the space for the women.

When the women heard that, they started crying. One of them said that she was relieved she would be able to breastfeed her son. My friend promised to try to find them a better place.

11 p.m. Complete darkness. I have never understood those who sleep with the lights on. In the past, I would turn off all the lights to sleep. Now, I hate the darkness, because it intensifies the feelings of fear, uncertainty and despair.

Hope is on my sister's lap, sleeping. We can't see each other. I am lying on the couch. I know how sad she is because we will leave him, but we both know this is the best for him. Out of nowhere, she starts talking to me.

'When you go tomorrow to see the guy, ask him to take care of Hope.'

'OK.'

'Tell him that the food we will give him is enough for a whole month; we will bring him more after that.'

'OK.'

'Tell him that we love him, and the only reason we are letting him go is for his own good.'

'Tell whom? The guy or Hope himself?'

Even though I couldn't see her, I knew she was crying.

Monday 8 January

2 p.m. After meeting Ahmad's friend, we head to meet his cousin for 'the interview', as he jokingly calls it. Ahmad's friend has never had a pet in his life, so he does not understand how important this meeting is for me. To be honest, it is not the act of giving Hope to another person that I find painful – in normal circumstances, we would have fostered him for a while and then found him a permanent home. It is the feeling of guilt. Am I leaving him alone?

On our way, Ahmad's friend sees two guys he met recently after they evacuated to his area. I discover later that one of them comes from a very wealthy family. They owned a building that was levelled to the ground.

They are laughing. The guy tells us the story: 'So all I have left – I mean *had* – were two pairs of trousers, two T-shirts, three pairs of underwear and three pairs of socks. I woke up this morning and could not find my clothes. I washed them last night and hung them out to dry. This morning, they were gone. After hours of searching, we reached the market, and I found out that someone had stolen my clothes and was selling them.'

I told him: 'Well, that is good, you got your clothes back.'

'No, I did not,' he said, laughing. 'The thief was a woman. So, when I wanted to go talk to her, my father stopped me, and he told me that this woman might be in a dire need to steal clothes and sell them. So we agreed to do something I never thought in my life I would do. I decided to buy my clothes back.'

The other guy was laughing so hard I thought he would have a heart attack.

'But guess what?' he says. 'By the time we reached her, another man had bought most of the stuff. But I was able to buy something.'

By now, the other guy was literally on the ground, laughing.

'I bought back my boxers. My used, worn boxer briefs. For twice their original price.'

At that moment, I realised how unfunny the story was. How this guy and his friend, who were laughing, were actually crying inside. I stopped smiling, looked at him and said: 'I'm so sorry for your loss. It must have been very difficult for you to go through that.'

They both went silent, and he said: 'Thank you for saying that.'

3 p.m. We enter Ahmad's cousin's home. I feel relieved to see a big area and surrounding trees. This means that Hope will have a beautiful space. We sit on the chairs outside, and they offer us tea.

The cousin is one of the kindest people you could meet. He is twenty years old and has three adorable cats himself. He was very nice, he asked about all the details related to Hope: health, food habits, etc. I thanked him for agreeing to take in a stray cat, but he was more than happy. He even refused to take any money for unexpected expenses, but I insisted.

On our way out, he put his hand out to shake mine, but instead I hugged him.

'Thank you,' I said. 'Thank you very, very, very much.'

I, a homeless person myself, displaced and not safe, was grateful that little Hope had found a home.

Tuesday 9 January

8 a.m. Am I still alive? Well, I am sure I'm still breathing; the pain all over my body is a sign that it is functioning. What does 'alive' mean? Is everything we are going through called 'life'? I wonder about the difference between me and a dead person. Does the loss of safety and your hopes and dreams qualify you to be dead? Because if so, this means that Gaza has become a city of ghosts.

Is it a life when you are helpless all the time, unable to even provide your loved ones with their basic needs?

In a phone call with my friend, whom I have been trying to reach for the past three months (wow! I cannot imagine it has been three months), she tells me that she and her family are still alive.

'My children always ask me for their favourite food and toys,' she tells me. 'I had to take them to the empty shops to show them that there is nothing left. I wanted badly to make them believe that I would sacrifice my whole life for a moment of safety and joy they could have, but there is nothing I can do.'

She tells me how, when she took her children out, she was holding them tightly to keep them safe and not lose them in the crowd. She talks about the huge numbers of people everywhere you go, and how the streets are packed. I share with her that a couple of weeks ago, I saw a lost little girl who was crying. She couldn't see her family, and hundreds of people were moving in all directions. I stood next to her and did not know what to do. I asked around if anyone knew her, but no one did.

About ten minutes later, a big man approached. He was almost taller than everyone in the street, and he had broad shoulders. He picked the girl up and put her over his shoulders and he kept turning around in a circle, until her sister, a teenager, who was at the end of the street, saw and came running towards us. He put the girl down, and she hugged her sister.

10 a.m. I go to check on my friend, and I get the chance to meet the family that is hosting him. They have the most adorable little girl. She is sociable and has a beautiful smile.

The family tells me that she hasn't gone out of the house for almost three months. The little girl tells me about her friend and how much she loves her. It turns out 'her friend' is actually a lady who lives in the building nearby. They have never spoken together, but when the lady goes to put out the laundry, the girl puts her head out of the window and waves at her, and the lady would smile back.

'So, do you have any other friends?' I ask.

She says the lady is her only friend. 'I love her.'

Later on, I met a 'friend' of mine. I have never met the man before, but it turns out that he used to work in the kitchen of one of my favourite restaurants. I am so glad to see him; he, somehow, is a connection to a life I no longer have. He tells me that he helped with preparing all the dishes and sweets, but his main task was the salads.

He and everyone around start talking about the situation: what to expect, the fear of the unknown future. I say: 'Can we please speak about something else, something positive?'

'Like what?' he asks.

'Like salads,' I say.

He laughs.

I ask: 'So tell me, what was the most popular salad? I used to order Greek salad or Caesar salad every time I had lunch at the restaurant. Also, you had the best molten cake in Gaza. I used to come especially to order it.'

I ask him if he cooks at his house, because I hear that chefs never do that after a long day of cooking. He says he cooks for his wife only. When they invited people over, they ordered takeaway.

He shares many stories about the restaurant, and on his way out he says he hopes we meet again. I tell him I will meet him one day in the restaurant and try one of his delicious salads.

1 p.m. It is time to take little Hope to his new home. My sister gives me a big bag that has wet food, dry food, his medicine and some cheese. He likes cheese. She has also put the only two toys she got from our home. They belonged to our cats; they are in the shape of a reindeer and Santa Claus. She says he needs them more than our cats.

I put him in the bag and get ready to go out, when she stops me. She takes him out and asks him for forgiveness and promises him that if he and we make it out alive, she will visit.

6 p.m. I receive a message from the guy who took Hope. He tells me that he is doing very well, and he sends me two photos. The photos take around two hours to open, but it is totally worth it. In one of them he is sleeping in his lap, and in the other he is chasing a ball.

I am grateful we found this angel to take care of him.

10 p.m. I have always been impressed by those who are eloquent with words, who have the capacity to express their inner thoughts precisely. I recall a message between me and a friend who lives abroad. I told her that the situation is getting worse. In her response, she put the word 'getting' into brackets. I understood what she meant; for three months the situation has been awful. But what English word to use after 'bad'? 'Worse'? 'Worst'? There are no stronger words to show that the situation continues to deteriorate.

Just when you think that you have hit rock bottom, you realise you were wrong. There is always a new low. Whether it is dignity-wise, basic-needs-wise or just living.

I miss a life where I would sleep on a bed, go to work, drink clean water, eat something I like of my own choice, meet friends and go back to the same bed and watch something online or read a book. I miss a life where mothers can walk in the streets and let their children run in front of them, enjoying the fresh air and, later, enjoying delicious foods and sweets. I miss a life where children have other children around, to play with, become friends, and to start creating beautiful memories for their future.

That life seems very distant and unrealistic. A fairy tale.

Saturday 13 January

8.30 a.m. We hear a lot of noises outside. Almost every member of our host family and the other families staying here is moving around. I get worried – did something bad happen? During the seconds that it takes my sister to go and open the door to see what is happening, my panicking mind goes through a whole plan: I will take this bag, we will get the cats. We cannot take anything else, no time to put shoes on.

My sister tells me that everything is OK. It seems that a woman and her children, who evacuated recently and had nothing with them, were knocking on doors and asking for help. So everyone starts going through their belongings and giving them anything they could share. I would not say 'anything they did not want or had a lot of', because this is a luxury we forgot about a long time ago.

I go out and see a pile of stuff: there are women's clothes, deodorant, tissues, sheets and some food cans. My sister gets cheese and some food as well. One of the other hosted family members whispers to the grandmother of the host family. They both look at the feet of the children, noticing the torn sandals they are wearing. Immediately, everyone goes inside and brings shoes for adults and children and adds them to the pile.

The grandmother asks the woman to give anything that does not fit to those around her in other tents. Before the woman and children leave, the grandmother goes inside again and brings some loaves and a few bottles of water. 'I wish I could give you more,' she says.

It all happens in front of me like a cinematic scene, everyone trying to help. No one stops for a second to question if they should keep something for themselves. On their way out, the grandmother asks the woman to come from time to time, maybe she could help her with something.

I ask the grandmother if she knows the woman, but she does not. What I admire most is the grandmother giving her the bread. These days, everyone is trying to maintain enough food to survive. She shares an old proverb that her own grandmother taught her: 'Bites deter hardships.' It means that food – that you feed to others, or any kind of help in general – will push away many bad situations and bad things around you. Any good you do will get back to you.

However, it startles me how my brain, in any normal situation, always thinks about the worst-case scenario. It feels like the blessing of having a normal life has been taken from us, for ever.

10 a.m. While I was out, a couple I know came by. My sister welcomed them. 'They did not stay long. They just passed by to give us the leftovers of two tins of canned meat,' she tells me. 'Since they know there are cats around us in the land, and they know how scarce food is to feed them, they decided to bring the leftovers to feed to the cats.'

I look at the leftovers, and the amount is enough to feed one cat. I am amazed, because I know that they are staying in a place that is relatively far away, which means they walked for a while to reach us, just to give us the food.

I go out of the house and find Moonlight. Moonlight is the deaf cat that my sister and her friend found and brought to stay in the nearby land. The neighbours are no longer surprised when they see my sister holding a cat and bringing it to the land.

I am grateful that Moonlight's food arrived for him, despite the small quantity. I am happy that some people are still thinking of animals, despite these extremely tough times.

2 p.m. I am sitting with a group of friends when a friend of theirs joins us. 'I have three daughters. The youngest one was eight months old when the whole nightmare started,' she says. 'Can you imagine that during these three months, she has learned how to crawl, then sit by herself, then walk? I wish I'd had the chance to film her when she walked for the first time, just like her two other sisters.'

Later on, everyone at the table starts sharing videos on their mobile phones of happy moments. One woman shares a video from her home while her family were dancing to music; I share a video from a friend's wedding party; another guy shares a video of his last trip. Then another woman picks up her phone and starts showing us the different meals that she used to make. Watching these makes us scream at least once or twice. I tell her that once this is all over, I am inviting myself to her house for three consecutive days to try the steak that her husband makes, the pasta she makes and the *maftool* (a traditional Palestinian dish) that her mother makes and sends to them.

245

I keep thinking about the many first moments that every one of us has lost, and the beautiful memories that were a reality three months ago. Yet now they are videos and photos of people I am not sure I could recognise any more.

6 p.m. Ahmad confides in us that the oldest grandchild has been upset, since she hasn't seen her friends in a long time. She also said that she wishes she could go out on trips like they used to.

I know that the girl likes to draw and colour, so I ask her if she would like us to draw something together.

Since there is no light, my sister turns on the torch on her tablet, and we start drawing. The girl suggests we draw a garden, a tree, the sun and flowers. While we are drawing, she asks me: 'Are there blue flowers? Because I want to use blue to colour one of them.'

'Of course there are,' I tell her. 'And even if there aren't, feel free to use any colour you want. It is your painting; be creative. And you know what? I will draw one flower on my side in blue.'

I pick up my phone and go through my photos, until I find pictures of some bouquets I have bought in the past. One of them has a blue flower that I show to her. She is surprised.

Manara the cat, who is staying with us tonight, comes and sits on my lap and starts watching us while we draw. The girl picks up the paper and asks Manara her opinion regarding colours and the number of flowers. She also asks her if she likes the painting, and we both agree that since she keeps looking at it, she does.

When we finish, she proudly shows my sister our painting. We start playing cards. Her mother comes in to check on her. She asks her if she is having a good time. The girl smiles and nods that she is.

After an hour and a half of painting, we start packing up, and she tells me how much she wishes to see a blue flower in person.

I tell her: 'When all of this is over, I promise that I will visit you and I will bring you a huge bouquet of flowers. And in the centre, there will be a blue one.'

She smiles, thanks me and my sister, and then leaves.

8 p.m. Lying on the couch, I think about everything that happened in the day. I think about the generosity of the host family in these hard times, how they are helping others when they themselves need help.

In these hard times, being kind is one of the most difficult things to do, but the host family and many people around me do it effortlessly.

I think of the father who could not enjoy the first time his daughter walked. And I wonder how many 'firsts' she will have that will not be celebrated.

I think of the many flowers I have received and given throughout the years. And I wonder: will I ever be able to fulfil my promise to the granddaughter?

Saturday 20 January

10 a.m. Over a hundred days have passed. Is anyone but us counting? In the past, I have always wondered about that moment when medical workers, especially doctors, start dealing with sick people as work and not as humans. Right now, I ask myself whether people around the world, witnessing and watching our misery, have reached the stage where they think of us as merely news instead of children with dreams for the future; mothers and fathers who wanted a better life for their kids; teachers who wanted to inspire the coming generations; and workers and farmers and musicians who wanted to follow their passion.

For the first time since this whole nightmare started, I went to the sea. I forgot how vast and blue it is. It was like meeting an old friend. Everywhere around was packed; people were everywhere. I bet if you took a photo from a bird's view, all you would see are big numbers of heads in the shape of dots, with few spaces available.

I sat on the sand and saw a big family by the shore. The women were filling buckets of water and washing dishes and dirty clothes, while the men went shirtless into the sea, with their trousers rolled up above the knees, to wash.

I saw a man and his son sleeping on a piece of cloth, right under the burning sun. I felt sorry for them that they had nothing to cover their faces with. I remembered a discussion I had with Ahmad about his continuous back pain from sleeping on the ground. He told me that having a roof over his head when he sleeps is a thousand times better than sleeping in a tent or being displaced in schools. He said that we are really blessed.

Ahmad keeps surprising me with his acts of kindness. A couple of days ago, he went out and gathered all the children and gave them balloons. He knows all the children, even the ones of the displaced families. And they and their parents know him. When he went up to his room, his niece knocked on the door several times to tell him that the children who did not get balloons had shown up. He gave her some to give to them.

On the shore, there were many people walking. I saw a couple holding hands. I think they are really strong. The fact that they have the ability to express their affection for each other during these horrible times is impressive. There were also children playing with kites, but not normal ones. They were kites made of sewing thread, and instead of pieces of cloth, they had actual notebook papers with homework written on them.

They say it is always about the perspective you have when you look at or observe a certain situation. At that moment, I looked at the whole scene from the perspective of an exhausted guy crushed by the cruelty of life. I couldn't see the beauty of the children playing, of the couple of lovers walking, of the acts of survival of displaced people to maintain the bare minimum standards of hygiene, nutrition or shelter. I saw only the empty gazes of people towards the nowhere. I saw sadness all over the place. I saw people with eyes full of tears. I saw those who are desperate for a moment of peace during these chaotic times.

I stayed for around two hours. Then I stood up and left.

12.30 p.m. On my way to the house of the host family, I passed by a pharmacy. I make sure to enter every pharmacy I find and ask for my medicine, and the different types of medicine that my friends or their families take. You never know when a pharmacy might get a couple of pills of any medicine. I ask the pharmacist about my medicine and expect that he will tell me that he does not have it, but I am wrong. He has one strip of it. I am very happy. I buy it, but on my way out, I go back and tell him that I still have some pills with me. I suggest that he cuts the strip in half and keeps the other half with him in case someone else asks for it. He smiles and says: 'Think only of yourself. In these times, it is all about survival.'

I don't agree with him. I insist that he takes half of it in case someone else asks for it.

I pass by a huge line of people waiting for bread. I guess the number on the men's side was over three hundred and, on the women's, two hundred. A guy I know tells me that if he can get bread for his family within five hours, he will be lucky.

2 p.m. I arrived at the house of my host family, to find four of my friends waiting for me. During the past couple of weeks, we have all run into each other on different occasions, and since then, we have started to meet and sit together. None of us had a strong relationship before with each other (except for a married couple), but our relationship has strengthened during these times. We chit-chatted for a while, until one guy said: 'Look at my shirt! Look at how wrinkled it is! One thing I wish to wear is an ironed shirt. I wish I could go back to the days when I used to take my clothes to the dry cleaner.' I remember my own dry cleaner, and how trusted he was. Several times, he gave me money I forgot in the pockets of my shirts or pants. I wonder where he and his family are now, and whether they are still alive?

The words of the guy kept repeating in my head; I really wanted to do something nice for him. So I got an idea. I went quickly and bought some coal. Coal is very expensive these days. It is the 'luxurious' alternative, rather than wood, to generate heat. I bought a few pieces, and when I got back, I asked the grandmother if she could help me heat them. She generously agreed. After that, I asked her to give me the smallest frying pan she has. The frying pan was big enough for one egg. I put the coal on the frying pan and then went back.

They all looked at me, wondering where I went. I said to the guy: 'Take off your shirt. I think we can make your dream of having an ironed shirt come true.' I laid the shirt on the couch and I started passing the heated frying pan over the shirt. After a long time and several trials, the shirt was 'ironed'. If you saw it in a normal context, you would never wear it, but compared to its old state, it was excellent. They were all laughing, encouraging me and, most importantly, asking me to be careful and not drop any coal on the shirt and ruin it. When I finished, he wore the shirt and was very happy.

One of the women shared a situation about how scarce clothes are. She looked for days for a hoodie. Finally, she entered a shop and found one – only one. 'The price was impossible. I refused to buy it. But then, only a few minutes later, I decided to get it, since I was afraid I wouldn't find anything else. I went back, and it was sold!'

After a while, one guy turned on a song by Umm Kulthum on his mobile. Umm Kulthum was an Egyptian singer who was given the title 'Star of the East'. She had such a strong voice, she sang to big audiences without a microphone. The surprising thing is that, even in times when people look only for the short songs and TV shows that you can binge-watch during the weekend, many of the younger generation still love listening to her hour-long songs, without feeling bored.

We were six people. When the song started, we started singing along and swaying to the music. For a moment, we forgot what was going on around us. We were just a group of friends, from all roads of life, enjoying some music.

On their way out, my sister hugged the women and thanked all of them for the fun time we had.

8 p.m. My stomach aches, my back hurts, my knees are killing me. I cannot stop thinking, and reminding myself, that right now I am living the best scenario anyone in Gaza is living. I am privileged to be under a roof, have access to some food and water, be around some nice people – and staying alive. Other people in Gaza dream of having half of what I do.

Still, I am not OK, I am not OK at all. I am the complete opposite of OK. I am sad, broken, hurt, humiliated and displaced.

I close my eyes, try to focus on the blue sea I saw today, and I pray for a better tomorrow.

Wednesday 31 January

3 a.m. The only thing worse than complete desperation is desperation mixed with hope. It is like someone is putting your head underwater to drown, and then they pull your head up for a couple of seconds to take a breath, then push it underwater again. That is what we are going through, one bitter moment after another, with a hint of positivity.

Wide awake, I couldn't stop thinking of all the tragedies we have been going through. It is like one of those TV shows that run for many seasons, and then, when the writers are out of ideas, they come up with an illogical scenario just to kill some characters off, introduce new ones and add some 'spice' to the series. It seems that the writers of my own show have gathered and thought to themselves: 'How could we make his life more interesting?' Someone jumped in and said: 'Well, what about we get him and his family displaced, with little food and other resources? What about putting everything he believes in to the test? Also, why only him? Why not write an event that would affect everyone around him?' It seems that this storyline was approved by the production team, and they went with it. All I hope for now is a couple of mundane episodes that could be easily skipped.

Out of all the reasons why I can't sleep, severe cold is the strongest. No matter what I do, it goes directly to my bones. I remember a few days ago, how heavy the rain was. When I went out, the water was running in the street, creating a barrier. You could go deep into water almost up to your knees. All I wanted was to take the few steps to reach the other side, but could not. So I decided to walk, hoping I would find a way across. I kept walking for a long time, until I reached an area far away. I saw a guy I know on the other side, trying to come into mine. We started screaming at each other.

'Isn't life funny?' he said. 'I want to come into your side, while you are trying to come into mine.'

'Do you remember those riddles about crossing the river?' I yelled. 'It seems that this is one of them.'

We kept walking until we reached an area where the water level was low and some people had placed big rocks for others to step on to cross. When he finally reached my side, I asked him what he was doing.

'Well, some of our relatives are staying in a tent,' he said. 'I want to go get them to stay with us until the rain is over.'

'Haven't you told me that you have seven families with you right now?'

'Yes, but we have no other option.'

I moved aside to let a man holding a child in his arms cross. I kept anxiously looking at him while he stepped over the rocks to the other side, hoping the child wouldn't fall. After he passed, I exchanged a few words with the guy and then crossed to the other side myself.

6 a.m. Manara is pregnant. Very pregnant. Her belly is big and she is sleeping a lot. Since she got pregnant, she has started going out less. There is a small tree in the nearby land that she loves sitting under. I have noticed that she yearns for female energy, whether it is my sister's, the grandmother's or the oldest granddaughter's. Once any one

254

of them is in the room, she goes and sits in their lap. These days, she is eating less, yet more often, and she drinks a lot. In my culture, when a woman is pregnant and she gets prettier, it means she is having a girl, but if the situation is otherwise, it means she is having a boy. It seems that Manara will have lots of girls.

Every time Manara goes out, she comes back with another stray cat from the street. 'I wonder if she goes outside just to bring stray cats to our room,' I said to my sister. 'It is like she is telling them there is a place where there is food and shelter.' We feed them a little and then let them out.

Finding food for the cats has become really difficult. The way we coordinate, search and call everyone to provide them with food seems irrational compared with the events we are going through. 'Those are first world problems,' someone once told me. 'People cannot have food these days, and you think about animals!' I know that, but those cats are our responsibility and feeding them is a priority.

My sister pointed out a terrifying fact. Manara went to mate almost two months ago, which means that she might deliver her babies very soon – one thing I don't think we could handle well. When she wanted to mate, we did our best to keep her inside; we were afraid that the whole nightmare wouldn't end before she gave birth, and we were right. However, she kept meowing and nagging, non-stop, day and night, which led us, after almost two weeks, to let her out.

I was walking in the street the other day when I saw a guy I knew. 'When we evacuated, my sister put our cat in a bag and ran with her,' he said. 'It all happened fast. She did not take clothes nor certificates. Only the cat.'

He continued: 'But my sister isn't the craziest one in our family. My father is. He took the hens with him, the hens! Can you imagine that? We were screaming, running, and he was collecting the hens to take with him. My family is out of this world.'

After a while, I asked him if they have food for the cat. He said: 'Yes, we do feed it any food leftovers or tuna, if available.' He was talking while I put my hand out to shake his, ready to leave. When our hands shook, he continued talking and said: 'We need to take care of the cat, she is blind.' I did not say a word. He smiled, but I did not. There is so much misery in this world. So much misery.

1 p.m. While waiting for a friend, I met a guy I know. He evacuated with his family from the north and is staying in a school. The women and children stay in one of the classrooms; over sixty persons share the room. He said they sleep so close to each other that they can't move. He and the men sleep downstairs in a tent.

'When we first got here, I stopped eating for almost a month,' he told me. 'I did not want to have to use the toilet. There is a long wait to get into the toilet, and at the beginning the toilet was filthy. But now, the displaced people work together to ensure it is hygienic all the time.'

He continued: 'Sleeping in the tent during these cold times is awful. Everyone is sick. I had a mattress but gave it to my older brother, who suffers from back pain. I put my head on the mattress while the rest of my body is off it.'

Next to us was a man selling some vegetables. A woman approached, yet she was hesitant. In our culture, people buy vegetables and fruit in kilos. But the woman took one tomato and asked him to weigh it and tell her the price. Then she added another tomato and did the same. After the seller told her the price, she opened the small money carrier she had and looked at what she had inside. Then she said that she will take one tomato only. The guy I was talking to went and added three tomatoes, gave them to the woman and paid the seller.

'You know what hurts the most?' he said. 'You wouldn't believe it. It is having to buy lemons. In our land, we had many big trees of lemon. We never had to buy any. All the neighbours and friends would come to us to take them. It is true that we lost our homes and everything we have. But losing those trees has had a deep effect on my soul. It is just too hard, too hard.'

He said that for the first time in his life, he thinks about leaving Gaza for ever. 'Even my mother is encouraging me to do so. She asked me, if we survive, to leave and never look back.'

When my friend came, I introduced them to each other. When he knew the guy has no mattress, he said: 'I think I could help. I know someone with an extra mattress.' The guy, shyly, offered to wait till tomorrow to go and get it, but my friend said we should go immediately. The happiness I saw on the guy's face when he held the mattress was unbelievable.

4 p.m. I saw a woman I know – we are not very close, but we are both close friends with another person. The mutual friend has left Gaza and is staying in a foreign country with some family members. After sharing greetings, she asked if it was possible to take a photo together and send it to our friend. I hesitated at first. I rarely take photos, because if we make it through these days alive, I do not want to have any reminder of them. I agreed, though – I put on a big smile and we took the photo. She said she will share it once she has access to the internet.

Two hours later, I received messages from our friend. She told me how happy she is with the photo and how amazing we look, which I doubt. She told me that she had a dream about the both of us the other day. We were at our favourite restaurant and we were going through the menu that we have already memorised by heart. 'We were very happy,' she wrote.

She also shared that she spends a lot of time in the library. 'There is nothing to do but watching the news and being worried for my loved ones. I go to the library and read. They have big libraries with lots of books. I am sure you would love it if you were here. But the people are not as sociable as we are. They don't speak a lot; they barely smile at you.'

Seeing her message brought tears to my eyes. I really miss her and all my friends.

8 p.m. I am sad, exhausted and frustrated. Minutes ago, my sister, Ahmad and I sat down and started sharing who, among the people we know, had died recently. A friend's mother, another friend's brother and a third friend's sister. The angel of death is roaming the skies of Gaza, non-stop.

It is very hard when your friends are going through tough times, yet you cannot be there with them to share their sadness. We are too tired to express sadness. I just want to sit in silence and grieve; I want to do nothing and talk to no one.

We heard knocking on the door. The oldest granddaughter peeked through the door and asked: 'Would you like to play cards?'

I looked at her, and then said: 'Sure, why not? Let's play cards.'

Saturday 3 February

8 a.m. A decision that you are forced to make is not a decision. That was my thought while my sister and I waited for the man who was coming to take Manara. It kills me that we are going to send her away, but we have no option. In addition to the fact that she is pregnant and might give birth soon – which is something we are not prepared for logistically or emotionally – her ruined eye still bleeds from time to time, which means she needs a surgical intervention the minute the whole nightmare is over.

The man who came to take her is somebody we fully trust: an animal lover, he never hesitates to save animals or do what is best for them. For over three months we did not have access to him due to the bad communications. Finally, we did, and he, despite being displaced with his family, is offering Manara all the care he can provide.

We did not give him Manara only, but two additional cats as well. The first cat I found the day before, and his back leg is broken. When I saw him in the street, I hoped he was just standing there, but on my way back, hours later, he was still in the same spot, so I brought him with me. The second cat is a kitten that appeared around a week ago out of nowhere. We couldn't find his mother.

I tried to speak to Manara, to apologise for letting her down and not taking care of her in the best way. As if she knew what was about to happen, she refused to even look at me, and she was very anxious. When the man showed up, he took one look at her and said: 'She will give birth within seven to ten days.'

The two other cats showed no resistance, yet Manara fought and meowed very loudly. She did not want to leave. She must have thought that we were abandoning her. We let her in, took good care of her, and now, at a very vulnerable situation – the last days of her pregnancy – we were letting her go with someone she did not know to an unknown destination. She must have thought we were the most horrible people in the world. She did not know how difficult the whole thing was for us. We needed a better chance for her and her babies. A chance we could not have guaranteed if she had stayed with us.

I don't know why, but the minute the car moved, the words of a friend played in my head. I got the chance to talk to her in mid-November, a month after the whole thing started. By then, she and her family had been displaced twice. She told me how she never physically disciplines her daughter, but when she does something wrong, she would take her tablet device away from her and not allow her to go visit her best friend.

'My daughter thinks that I am punishing her,' my friend said. 'She begs me to see her friend or give her her stuff that we left behind in our house when we evacuated. I have tried to explain to her over and over that she has not done anything wrong. But her little mind can't grasp what is actually happening. I feel extremely guilty.'

My heart aches, for Manara, for my sister, my friend and her daughter, and for every person who suffered and is still suffering.

Noon For over three months, the main means of transportation has been by animals or on foot. There are few cars on the streets. In addition to the fact that movement has become very difficult due to the huge number of people in the streets, fuel is very expensive.

To take a taxi has become a unique experience. I couldn't believe that I was in a car. Today, I asked the driver about what he uses for fuel. He told me there are two options these days. The first is using gas canisters; and the other option is a mixture of fuel and cooking olive oil. The drivers would mix three litres of cooking olive oil with one litre of fuel.

'Filling a gas canister is very difficult, but what is the canister for if I don't have food to cook with it?' the driver, who has been displaced with his family for almost four months, told me. 'All our money is gone. If you had little money on you at the beginning, it is gone now. At least I can provide a few things to my family with the money I get from the car.'

I asked him whether the two alternatives are safe. He said: 'Neither is safe nor good for the car. They ruin the motor. But what other option do we have? All we want is to survive, and after this is over, I can deal with the car issues.'

It goes without saying that the prices to travel by car are expensive, and you take four to five times the required time, due to the heavily crowded streets.

3 p.m. Another friend tells us that he had an argument with his host family, which led to him moving out. Every now and then, the same scenario happens, over similar details. It has been four months now, four long months.

I can never blame any host family for asking people to leave. Hosting another family means more food consumption, less space, more stress, less stability. After all this time, having disagreements, disputes and problems is the normal result. Everyone is stressed out, everyone is not OK, everyone is extremely upset.

I contacted a friend to check on her. Her family were staying at her best friend's house. 'We had to move,' she said. 'Things got really bad, and I don't want to lose my best friend over this. Half of my family went to the house of my father's friend, while the rest, including myself, are staying in a tent.'

For the last three months at least, finding a separate place is almost impossible, and if you are super lucky, you will have to pay crazy amounts of money. Days ago, a friend of mine told me they found an empty apartment that has only walls (no kitchen or utilities like basins, taps, etc.). The owner asked for $1,400 a month and three months' payment in advance.

Our host family are incredible people; they have never made us feel unwelcome, even at the worst of times. But I am always terrified that something might happen, and we will be asked to, or have to, leave before this is all over.

11 p.m. I want to use the toilet. I go outside, pass by the many bodies sleeping on mattresses, trying to make the least noise possible. I open the toilet door, and I hear some rattling. It is complete darkness, so I turn on the flashlight I have and see a mouse moving.

I walk backwards and close the door. For the past four months, I have always done my best to pass through the hallway without looking around, to respect the privacy of the people. For the first time, I look around, trying to locate where Ahmad is sleeping.

Most people have their faces under their blankets. It is very cold these days. I find Ahmad, and he turns his face towards me.

'Ahmad, wake up,' I whisper.

'I am awake, don't worry. Is something wrong?'

'There is a mouse in the toilet.'

'OK. Just keep the door closed, and someone will deal with it the first thing next morning.'

I want to yell that I need to use the toilet, and I would never do it with a mouse inside. But I do not want to disturb people. So I go back to the room and sit on the couch, covering myself with my blanket and wearing all the clothes I have, including my jacket. I keep thinking of all the decisions 'I took' that I never wanted to.

I never wanted to leave my apartment, yet I made the decision to leave.

I never wanted to stop taking my medicine regularly, yet I am doing so.

I never wanted to wear the things I am wearing now for five days in a row; to eat what I am eating now; to sleep on a couch; to walk for hours to find basic things. But I made the decision to do all of these things.

I never wanted to let Manara go, but I made the decision to do so.

I did not want to go back to the room without having used the toilet, but I went back.

I really want to have a simple, quiet life in which I am in control of the basic things related to myself. Right now, all I need, desperately, is the freedom to use the toilet.

Thursday 8 February

2 a.m. I have been sick for almost a week. I haven't been able to leave the mattress on the ground I have been sleeping on, except to go to the toilet. Due to new members joining the host family, some changes were made, and I gave them the couch I was sleeping on to take outside. Now, I sleep on a mattress so thin that I forget sometimes it exists.

My body has simply decided to fail me and not resist any more. Every part of it is aching, and the fever refuses to leave me. My friend checks on me via a message and says that she sends me all the love in the world. In the past, I used to believe that love makes miracles. But can love really end our suffering? Can it get me out of my sickness, to find that I am back to my house, my street and my life?

All I want is to sleep for half an hour, only half an hour.

8 a.m. My friends come to check on me.

'It is definitely because of the bad and expired food we have been consuming,' one says. Unfortunately, my friend is right, there are many things we eat that have passed their expiration dates, but what other option do we have? In the past, we would have never bought something that had less than one month left; now, we consume it gladly. Also, if you find a half-rotten piece of fruit or vegetable, you pretend it is not and eat the good part.

My other friend looks at him and says: 'Aren't we all expired? Our bodies still function, yet our hearts, brains and souls have expired a long time ago. So why not be feeding

266

this body expired food?' He answered in a joking manner, yet misery came out of every word.

Before leaving, the married couple tells us that they are planning to start selling sweets in the street. They say that half of the ingredients are not available, and the remaining half are super expensive. But they want to try, hoping they can make a little money to keep surviving. They have no money left after almost five months without work. We all encourage them and wish them luck, saying we will be their first customers.

11 a.m. I get to talk with my friend who is abroad: 'I die every day thousands of times thinking about my loved ones and my family members in Gaza. My mother, who must go through kidney dialysis three times a week, has the chance to have half a session every ten days. Now, she even refuses to go to the hospital. She is tired of waiting and the humiliation she faces.'

Noon My sister's friend showed up. He loves helping others, so he goes to areas where displaced people have set their tents to help. Sometimes with food, other times with stuff they need, or even by directing them to available services.

He told us about a young girl who asked him for something to eat. At that moment, he did not have anything edible on him, so he promised to bring her something the next time he visits. My friend stopped for a while, and then said: 'She looked at me and said that many people come and promise her, her family and all the others with things, but they never come back. I went to the car and cried my eyes out. Why on earth is this child and many others suffering? I did not leave until I was able to bring some food to her and the other children around.'

Then he shared with us an audio that his cousin, who lives abroad in an Arab country, sent him. His cousin said that many people don't even know what is going on in Gaza. They don't follow the news, and they become surprised when they hear about the suffering we are going through.

4 p.m. When you are sick and unable to move, you have a lot of time on your hands. Before my sister's friend left, he shared with me some movies he has on his mobile. The minute I saw the list, I knew that we do not share the same taste. However, I found a movie that I want to watch: *A Man Called Otto*, starring Tom Hanks. This movie is based on a novel by one of my favourite writers, Fredrik Backman. The original book is called *A Man Called Ove*. I would buy any book if I saw Backman's name on the cover.

In my apartment, I left many unread books, some by Fredrik Backman. Even before the whole nightmare started, getting books was not easy. We do have libraries (or now it should be we did have libraries) in Gaza, but only few options of books were available. I would ask my friends who travel abroad to buy me books.

I loved the movie and I loved Tom Hanks's performance. People could think of many works by Hanks but, for me, it is always *Forrest Gump*, and somehow this movie showed me the old Tom Hanks that I love. Also, the team has done great work to reflect the contents of the story, yet I always believe that a movie can never be as good as the book.

7 p.m. A guy I know calls to check on me. His wedding was supposed to be in December, but all his plans went south. I ask him about his fiancée, and to my surprise, he tells me they will get married in the coming days. He did not mean a wedding party, he meant that she will move from the tent she and her family are displaced in to the tent he and his family are in.

'She is devastated, and so am I. We both wanted a big wedding that I saved enough money for. I, secretly, was coordinating with her friends to prepare many surprises for her. I wanted to bring her the biggest bouquet of flowers, to dance and sing with her and tell her how much I love her. But our houses are gone, many members of our families and friends are dead, and we are away from each other. Her family members go out all day to find food and provide basic needs, and she stays alone, which is very unsafe. So we reached the decision, she, I and her father. We have no other option.'

8 p.m. A common, shy question I keep receiving: 'Do you have food? Do you have clothes?' Many people don't, and I am lucky to have access to some. Sometimes I wish someone would ask me: 'Do you have enough love around you? Do you have enough kindness?'

We are near Valentine's Day. I bet there is a couple celebrating their wedding, unlike my friend, whose wedding will be moving from one tent to another for safety. One person will send a huge box of chocolates to a lover, while here, in Gaza, people are searching non-stop for something to eat.

I bet there is a partner in one area of the world, angry at their lover and asking them to pay more attention to their emotional needs. Well, here in Gaza, I don't think we have this issue right now, because we have no time, energy or the privilege to think about what we feel.

Right now, all that we want is to be safe. Just safe.

Monday 19 February

8 a.m. I once read that you are 'as old as you feel'. I guess there are no children nor youth left in Gaza if we apply this equation. We have turned into a place of old people, waiting silently for a miracle to happen or for death to select them. Every day, every moment, our souls are getting older.

The kids have gotten really old recently. Physically, after almost five months of staying with the host family, the grandchildren are much taller. But it is not their bodies that grabbed my attention, it is their innocence that I see being stolen from them day after day. They are traumatised, they have lost friends and they haven't had a normal life in a long time.

I was on my way out when I saw the youngest grandchild holding a piece of bread in her hands. I asked her if she was going down to see the other kids in the street. 'Not until I finish my bread,' she said. 'My mother told me that not all children have enough bread. And if I go down and eat in front of them, some might feel sad.'

We both paused for a couple of seconds, until she asked: 'I do what my mother tells me, but why don't all children have bread?'

I stood there, startled by her question. Then she saved me by adding to her thought: '. . . and chocolate and potato chips and cotton candy and . . .'

She started counting all the fun, delicious things that children eat. Then a couple of cats came up, and she started telling me what each one of them did the previous day.

271

Apparently, one of them approached her sister while she was playing, and she patted him.

I said goodbye to her and left.

10 a.m. I see a man selling one pack of nappies. That is all he has to sell, a pack of nappies. For $73. Nappies have become a hidden treasure these days. They are scarce and they have become super-expensive if you find any. I remember once a friend of mine, who had his first baby, telling me about his shock with the many expenses of having a new baby: 'Every week, you need to buy a new packet of nappies and a can of powdered milk for your child.'

If parents are expected to get four packs each month, these days this means they need to pay over $280 [£230] just to ensure their babies are clean. Some people I know are using cloth pieces, but they say they are not practical at all.

The list of impossible prices goes on, including sugar. One kilo of sugar used to cost less than $1; last month it reached almost $8–9; yesterday it was $23.

A few steps away from the man, I see another guy selling things in the street. His face looks familiar, but I can't identify him. Minutes later, I realise why. Because I never thought that I would see a law graduate, a top student, in the middle of the street selling cans of beans and peas. I approach him, and he looks embarrassed, but I put the biggest smile over my face and tell him how happy I am to see him.

He is out of words and shy. 'Well, you know, everyone needs money these days, and right now, practising law is not an option.' He tries to say it in a joking manner. I remember that he was in the final stage of training at a law office, before getting the official licence. (In Gaza, after you finish studying law, you need to be an intern for two years before you get the licence to start practising on your own.)

I tell him that I am proud that he is trying his best to feed himself and his family. I buy some cans from him and tell him that I wish to see him after this whole nightmare is over.

I keep walking, and see something that I never would have imagined seeing, not even in these horrible days. With tents now taking up so much land, people are setting them on the pavements. How come a family would be able to sit, sleep and 'live' in such a narrow space, with all the chaos around? How can they feel safe with people actually walking around all the time, when anyone could easily enter the tent? One tent had a piece of carton on it, saying: 'There are displaced people inside. Please, do not try to peek or enter.'

4 p.m. The grandmother comes into our room to check on us. She is concerned after noticing that we haven't been eating well for almost two weeks.

I don't understand the pattern with which I, psychologically and physically, have been reacting to the whole thing. At the beginning, I stopped eating and lost lots of weight, then there was a stage where I ate anything I could find, and now I haven't been eating well. Sometimes I am full of hope and optimism for the future; others I am full of despair and sadness. It is like a turmoil.

As for the grandmother, I cannot imagine that she still has the energy to check on us, even though she never rests.

From the first hours of the day until the last ones, she will be cleaning, making food out of what is available, taking care of the children, fixing problems, helping others. And most of all, she never complains. In fact, she is the only person I have interacted with in the last five months who never complains.

She is such a great and strong woman.

9 p.m. Manara gave birth! After many trials over the past week to reach the man who took Manara, the phone finally rang. I was terrified of what he might tell us. I was terrified that he would say she ran away or that something bad had happened.

'She is next to me,' he said. 'She gave birth to three kittens. Approximately. I will send you a picture once I have an internet connection.'

I was very happy and kept thanking him over and over. The phone call was cut, and we couldn't reach him again. I was so grateful that I did not ask him what he meant by 'approximately'. My sister told me that maybe not all the kittens made it alive and that only three survived.

I opened the door, and without going out, in order not to invade the privacy of the host family, I shared with them the news. Sounds of joy came from their side, and the oldest grandchild came running towards me while clapping.

I will never forget how welcoming and kind this family is.

Midnight My close friend who lives abroad shares with me this message: 'Saw this and thought of you. It's what I've been trying to express: *If only I could, I would absorb your pain and return it to you as love.* A quote by Louise Kaufmann.'

Her message felt like a warm hug. I laid my body over the mattress, with a smile over my face. Hoping one day I will be safe, and I will see my friend, and we will have breakfast together and walk by the beach.

One day.

Saturday 2 March

2 a.m. I cannot take her words out of my head: the way she sounded well throughout the first part of our conversation, and then how her voice was full of tears.

'I went to check on my mother, and I found her crying. When I asked her about the reason, she looked at me and said: "I am hungry. Very hungry."'

My friend, a wonderful woman and mother of four young men, stayed with her family in the north. For five months I had tried to reach her, but failed. I couldn't believe my eyes when I saw her number on my mobile.

'Oh my God, you are alive! Alive!' I said.

'And you are, too!' she replied.

After a while, I dared to ask her about whether there is food and water available. She told me they haven't had a vegetable in five months; that a small amount of flour costs hundreds of dollars; and how hard the situation has been for her and her family.

When she spoke about her mother, she couldn't keep a steady, happy tone of voice and started crying. She told me that she wishes she could give her everything she wants. She shared with me that one time, they were able to secure enough flour to prepare one loaf of bread for each of her sons.

'My sons ate half of their loaves and brought me the remaining halves, telling me it is for their grandmother. My youngest (eleven years old) told me his two halves were not even, but he decided to give her the bigger one.'

276

When she asked me how we are doing, I couldn't complain about the lack of food, or the high prices, or the diseases, or the stress we are going through, because I knew that whatever we (those who moved south) have been through, they have gone through much worse.

At the end of the conversation, she tried to joke: 'My husband has always wanted to lose weight, yet he couldn't. In the previous five months, he has lost over 35kg [5st 7lb]!'

Before we ended our phone call, I told her how much I hope to see her again. I told her that whenever I think of her, I remember the video she posted, reacting to her eldest son's results in high school. In Gaza, all high-school students go through general unified exams that they must pass to enrol into universities. There was a trend on social media to document the minute they received their results, while showing the reaction of their proud parents. I remember how she jumped in the air, eyes full of tears and joy, and how she and her husband hugged their son.

Another thing I will always remember is the day she came to me and told me that she and her husband had been finally able to pay the first instalment for their new home. A home, unfortunately, they had to evacuate from.

8 a.m. I have been avoiding everything recently. Going out, talking to people and 'living' in general. I stay in the room and do nothing. I am tired of everything that is going on around me, of how inhumane and miserable our life is. My goal for each day is for its hours to finish and to cross it off the calendar. I want the hours and days to pass, until we

reach a moment where we are told that this nightmare is over.

I wondered if what I am going through is depression, but then I kicked the idea away because of that little, yet strong, seed of hope I have in my soul that, whenever it flies away due to the hard times we are going through, finds its way to land back over my heart and pushes me to have positive thoughts and wish for a better future.

One time, I was watching an episode of a TV show called *Killing Eve*, when one of the characters said: 'Grief makes us strangers, even to ourselves.' Even though the sentence was mentioned briefly, without any focus on it in the episode, it stuck in my head. I guess what I am going through is grief, but a different kind of grief. One mixed with stress, fear, loss and severe sadness.

My plan of isolation is cut from time to time, when I go to get, or do, something important. This time, it was about little Hope, the cat we found in the street. I received a message from the guy who has been hosting the cat for over a month now. He told me that he couldn't keep him any more. His message terrified me because I was not sure we will be able to find another home for him.

I started calling everyone I know. 'You do know that complete families are displaced, without a shelter, not even a tent, to protect them?' a friend said. 'And you are looking for a place for the cat?'

A couple of friends offered to take him in, but both went to consult with their spouses – and both returned back with negative results (their spouses were afraid of cats and refused). Another friend introduced me to a man who said he was willing to take him in but asked for a monthly allowance, and we couldn't agree on a price, so it did not work out.

Finally, a friend told me that her relative, whose family is displaced with hers in the same place, wants to take him in.

I went to get Hope and was so happy to see him: he has gotten bigger, and is still energetic and happy. The guy had really taken great care of him; he even returned the money we gave him and gave me some food as well.

While waiting for him to bring Hope, I got the chance to talk to his brothers and cousins, who were standing downstairs. One of them mentioned how much he misses eating fruit. They started counting types of fruits that they want to eat. Even though it is not my favourite, not even in my top five, I found myself telling them how much I miss eating guava. In fact, what I really missed was the smell of guava, rather than eating it. I also told them that I have this dream of eating strawberry ice cream one day.

When I arrived at the new family's location, over fifteen children came out and gathered around me. They were the sons and daughters of all the displaced people staying there. They were excited, saying: 'Our new cat is here. Please, let us touch him.' I talked to the woman who agreed to take Hope, shared some pieces of advice and left.

I was afraid Hope would be scared with the big crowd, but my friend told me that he is a 'strong little fella' who acts as if the new place has been his for ages. I was grateful to hear that.

8 p.m. Ahmad comes into the room to check on us. He is surprised I got out of the room today. We talk about music. He speaks about his favourite singers and songs. He loves an Egyptian song called 'My Beautiful Country'. He thinks that a current singer is the owner of the song, but I tell him that it is a cover. He surprises me when he tells me he does not know the original singer.

'Dalida? Who is Dalida?'

'Dalida was a world-famous singer and actor born in Egypt, but who rose to fame in Europe in the seventies. Then she went back to Egypt and started singing in Arabic.'

I search in my mobile and find the original song. It is a nostalgic one about the home country, the first love there and hoping that one day she will return. It is the first time I have listened to the song in the last five months, and this time, it feels completely different.

I think of my apartment, which is less than an hour away from me by car, as a faraway place that I wish to go back to one day. I scroll through my photos to see pictures of a life I used to have that no longer exists. It breaks my heart.

After Ahmad leaves, I start looking for other songs by Dalida on my mobile. I play my favourite one – a French song called 'Je suis malade' by Serge Lama, which she covered. Such songs made me believe in the importance of the written word; how the writer was able to describe the extreme sadness they were going through after losing their loved one. In the song, she says that being away from her loved one is similar to when her mother left her in the evenings, alone with her despair; that being away from him is like being an orphan in a dormitory.

In a weird way, I relate to the lyrics more than ever. I do feel left alone, like a little boy, scared of what the future is holding for me, missing a home and a complete life full of friends and beautiful details, gone in the blink of an eye.

But unlike the song, which starts by saying, 'I do not dream any more,' I do still have dreams. I dream of taking a hot shower, of eating strawberry ice cream and being safe.

It is that seed of hope. That stubborn, little, strong seed of hope.

NOTES

Introduction:
'Silence for Gaza' by Mahmoud Darwish, in *Journal of an Ordinary Grief* (1973)

Wednesday 18 October:
'Nassam Alayna El Hawa' by Fairuz, written by the Rahbani brothers (1968)
'Immortality' by Clare Harner (1934)

Saturday 28 October:
'Yemken Nesi' by Faia Younan, written by Adnan Azrouni (2019)

Tuesday 31 October:
'Think Upon Others' by Mahmoud Darwish (date unknown)

Sunday 5 November:
'Seven Small Ways in Which I Loved Myself This Week' by Sabrina Benaim, in *Depression & Other Magic Tricks* (Button Poetry, 2017)

Wednesday 8 November:
'Adam and Hanan' by Majida El Roumi, in *The Other*, directed by Youssef Chahine (1999)

Sunday 12 November:
Extremely Loud & Incredibly Close by Jonathan Safran Foer
    (Penguin, 2005)

Tuesday 14 November:
'Fi 7eta Tanya' by Abdel Basset Hamouda, written by Menna
    El Kiey, in *For Zeko*, directed by Peter Mimi (2022)

Friday 1 December:
The Perks of Being a Wallflower by Stephen Chbosky (Simon
    & Schuster, 1999)
I Know Why the Caged Bird Sings by Maya Angelou
    (Random House, 1969; Virago, 1984)

Thursday 7 December:
'Pack the Bags' by Iyad Rawami, on *Silence in Syria*
    compilation (2016)

Wednesday 20 December:
'You've Got Time' by Regina Spektor (Sire Records, 2014)

Sunday 31 December:
The Five Wounds by Kirstin Valdez Quade (W. W. Norton,
    2021)

Monday 19 February:
'If Only' by Louise Kaufmann (2023)